Within these pages you will find some surprising facts, as well as have some of your hunches about church growth confirmed. Anyone wanting to reach the growing unchurched population of today will do well to saturate themselves in the lessons Barna presents—lessons drawn from two years of researching the unchurched.

BILL EASUM
PRESIDENT, EASUM, BANDY AND ASSOCIATES

George Barna is a seemingly endless source of insight and assistance for keeping us in touch with the "real world" of our present day. Once again, he is helping us.

DR. JACK HAYFORD
CHANCELLOR, THE KING'S COLLEGE AND SEMINARY

"These are not the good old days," George Barna says—and he's right! These are "good days," full of opportunity to help people get connected to God, to the Church and to opportunities to make a difference in the world. This latest product of Barna's research will help you make the most of ministry opportunities today.

BRIAN MCLAREN
PASTOR, CEDAR RIDGE COMMUNITY CHURCH

With exact analysis and practical solutions, George Barna again serves the evangelistic mission of the Church.

LUIS PALAU
INTERNATIONAL EVANGELIST

Again George Barna has served the Church, this time through the careful research produced in *Grow Your Church from the Outside In*. His perspective is at such an altitude that it helps us truly get the big picture of why the unchurched are not attending churches, who they are and how best to get their attention. Not only is there data in this new book, but George's extrapolations are insightful. This book is an outstanding tool to help Church leadership bring their particular local congregation to a point of relevancy to the unchurched community.

TOM PHILLIPS
VICE PRESIDENT OF TRAINING, BILLY GRAHAM EVANGELISTIC ASSOCIATION

In his book *Grow Your Church from the Outside In*, George Barna gives us tremendous insights into how unchurched people think and what motivates them. This book is an invaluable resource if you are looking for practical strategies to enable your ministry to attract and retain unchurched people.

STEVE RUSSO
COHOST, *LIFE ON THE EDGE*

Once again George Barna has provided church leaders with a practical tool for assessing our strategy and success in reaching unchurched people. This is not a work filled with opinions of an individual church leader. In *Grow Your Church from the Outside In*, Barna gives us an up close look at the attitudes and perceptions of those we are failing to reach.

ANDY STANLEY
FOUNDER AND PASTOR, NORTH POINT COMMUNITY CHURCH

In *Grow Your Church from the Outside In* George Barna explains the reasons why the unchurched do not associate with our churches. If the Church can recognize who it is they are trying to reach and why the unreached do not want to be reached, then the Church might do a better job of reaching them with the gospel. A must-read for every pastor.

DR. ELMER TOWNS
DEAN, LIBERTY UNIVERSITY
AUTHOR, *WHAT EVERY SUNDAY SCHOOL TEACHER SHOULD KNOW*

GROW
YOUR CHURCH
FROM THE
OUTSIDE
IN

GEORGE BARNA

Regal

From Gospel Light
Ventura, California, U.S.A.

Published by Regal Books
From Gospel Light
Ventura, California, U.S.A.
Printed in the U.S.A.

Regal Books is a ministry of Gospel Light, an evangelical Christian publisher dedicated to serving the local church. We believe God's vision for Gospel Light is to provide church leaders with biblical, user-friendly materials that will help them evangelize, disciple and minister to children, youth and families.

It is our prayer that this Regal book will help you discover biblical truth for your own life and help you meet the needs of others. May God richly bless you.

For a free catalog of resources from Regal Books/Gospel Light, please call your Christian supplier or contact us at 1-800-4-GOSPEL or www.regalbooks.com.

Revised edition. Originally published as *Re-Churching the Unchurched* by Issachar Resources in 2000.

Cover and interior design by Robert Williams
Revised edition edited by Steven Lawson

Library of Congress Cataloging-in-Publication Data

Barna, George.
  Grow your church from the outside in / George Barna.— Rev. ed.
      p. cm.
Rev. ed. of: Re-churching the unchurched. 2000.
Includes bibliographical references (p.   ).
  ISBN 0-8307-3087-7 (hardcover)
  ISBN 0-8307-3075-3 (paperback)
  1. Evangelistic work. I. Barna, George. Re-churching the unchurched.
II. Title.
  BV3790 .B329 2002
  254' .5—dc21   2002008956

1   2   3   4   5   6   7   8   9   10   11   12   13   14   15   /   09   08   07   06   05   04   03   02

Rights for publishing this book in other languages are contracted by Gospel Light Worldwide, the international nonprofit ministry of Gospel Light. Gospel Light Worldwide also provides publishing and technical assistance to international publishers dedicated to producing Sunday School and Vacation Bible School curricula and books in the languages of the world. For additional information, visit www.gospellightworldwide.org; write to Gospel Light Worldwide, P.O. Box 3875, Ventura, CA 93006; or send an e-mail to info@gospellightworldwide.org.

CONTENTS

Foreword 9
By Lee Strobel

Acknowledgments 11

Preface 13

Chapter 1 15
The Crowd Awaits

Chapter 2 21
Sizing Up the Unchurched

Chapter 3 29
Why People Avoid Church

Chapter 4 39
A Demographic Profile of the Unchurched

Chapter 5 51
Values, Attitudes and Lifestyles

Chapter 6 69
The Faith of the Unchurched

Chapter 7 89
What the Unchurched Want from a Church

Chapter 8 109
Grabbing Their Attention

Chapter 9 127
Twelve Misconceptions About Ministry to the Unchurched

Chapter 10 141
How Churches Minister Effectively to the Unchurched

Chapter 11 158
Making a Commitment to a Vision of the Church

Appendix A 165
Research Methodology

Appendix B 168
About George Barna

Appendix C 169
About the Barna Research Group, Ltd.

Appendix D 171
The Christian Leader Profile

Appendix E 173
A Glance at the Unchurched

Bibliography 175

FOREWORD

Those of us who care passionately about seeing churches become more effective in evangelism can learn a lot from how President George W. Bush *didn't* respond to the terrorist attack on September 11, 2001.

He didn't merely increase the military budget by 3 percent, ask Americans to become a little more vigilant and send a sternly worded e-mail to those responsible for the aggression. Instead, he went on national television to declare war on terrorism and call for an immediate, massive and well-coordinated national response to the threat.

The truth is that churches face a spiritual enemy who is far more potent than terrorists from the Middle East. Eternal destinies are at stake—and by most measurements we are losing the battle. Yet many churches have responded by increasing their evangelism budget by 3 percent, asking their congregation to be a little more vigilant to evangelistic opportunities and forming another committee to possibly think about maybe planning an outreach event of some sort at an undetermined date in the future.

We must do more than that! We should declare war—and launch an immediate, massive and well-coordinated response so that an unprecedented number of people will come to faith in Jesus Christ.

If we are going to fight a winning evangelistic battle, we need intelligence. We must understand the task ahead of us so we can determine the best approach to reaching people with the life-changing and eternal-altering gospel of Christ. That is why George Barna's provocative and helpful new book, *Grow Your Church from the Outside In*, is so important.

Once again, Barna has performed a valuable service by conducting strategic research about the unchurched. All pastors who are interested in ratcheting up the evangelistic effectiveness of their churches—and that ought to be *all* pastors—should take advantage of this resource to help them shape their battle plans.

So analyze Barna's new data. Weigh his insights. Study other research. Learn lessons from your own relationships with the unchurched. Pray for guidance. Work with others in your church to fashion the kind of outreach efforts that will truly penetrate your community for Christ.

Then declare all-out war on evangelistic lethargy—and see what God does.

Lee Strobel
Author
Inside the Mind of Unchurched Harry and Mary,
The Case for Christ and *The Case for Faith*

ACKNOWLEDGMENTS

Although I write every word on every page, writing a book is never a solo effort. Many people work behind the scenes to make such an endeavor possible. I would like to briefly but sincerely thank many of the individuals who facilitated the birthing of this book.

Our friends at the North American Mission Board (NAMB) of the Southern Baptist Convention have consistently focused on reaching the unchurched. They graciously allowed me to use portions of the research that we conducted for them—and that they paid for—in this book. I am grateful for their generosity, for their partnership and for their modeling service to the kingdom. Any interpretations or statements in this book do not necessarily reflect their position or views.

My colleagues at the Barna Research Group not only worked with me to gather the research data on which this book is based, but to also free me from the tyranny of running the operations of the company. I am especially indebted to David Kinnaman, who has helped bring the company to a new level, largely without my interference. Rachel Ables somehow managed the editing, design, production and distribution of this book while also juggling all of our seminar and resource marketing activities. The rest of the core team provided invaluable assistance in this and the myriad of other projects in which we were also involved: those teammates include Chris Daradics, Kristen Daradics, Pam Jacob, Jill Kinnaman, Carmen Moore, Sarah Polley, Irene Robles, Celeste Rivera and Meg Wells. I have been blessed with a young, talented and vision-driven team that is contributing value to the kingdom.

I am grateful for the editing assistance of Julie Carobini, too. Someday I will learn the rules related to hyphens and semicolons. But not this week.

I appreciate the perseverance of Kim Wilson, who directs the activities of the Barna Institute. In spite of my consistently ignoring her while I wrote this book, Kim kept the wheels rolling with energy, joy and wisdom.

As always, my family has made the greatest sacrifices during this time of writing. My wife, Nancy, played every role during this burnout period, doing the homeschooling, cooking, house cleaning, taxiing, playing, Bible reading, praying—you name it, she master-minded it in order to free me up to prepare this resource for the Church. My wonderful daughters, Samantha and Corban, regularly checked on my progress and prayed for me (and with me) every day. There is nothing as encouraging as having a loving, caring, supportive family; I thank the Lord for providing me with one. And I pray that He will repay them for their sacrifices.

Thank you, each of you listed here, for your blessings to me.

And you, reader, can make it all worthwhile by taking the information contained in this book and using it to bless others, to fortify the Church, and to honor God. I wrote it for you, for that purpose.

PREFACE

Penetrating today's unchurched population may require an approach that differs from any that has been taken in the past. This book is based on two years of research conducted with several thousand unchurched adults and teenagers randomly selected from across the country. Using statistics and answers given during the extended interviews we conducted, I will try to explain that in many ways the unchurched are similar to believers, but in some other important ways they are also significantly different. The same strategies and experiences that may have encouraged us to become involved in church life may have no relevance to the needs, expectations, aspirations and lifestyles of today's unchurched. We will have to apply discernment and be wise as we approach them. We cannot compromise what we stand for simply to attract a lot of people, but neither can we lose our compassion for them.

Each chapter opens with a question. See how well you know the unchurched by answering the question before you read the chapter. I think you may be surprised by the real answers.

TWO-THIRDS OF ALL AMERICANS BELIEVE THAT THE PURPOSE OF LIFE IS TO

A. make a significant contribution to society.

B. have children and raise a family.

C. enjoy blessings and gain the maximum fulfillment from their options and temptations.

D. fulfill the destiny God has for them.

E. be a good person.

F. win the lotto.

CHAPTER 1

THE CROWD AWAITS

I love the closing portion of Acts 2, which describes the beginning of the Christian Church, just after Pentecost. Every time I read this passage I wonder who would *not* want to be part of such a community of faith. They spent time together learning about God, enjoying each others' presence, and serving other people. They took care of each other physically, emotionally and spiritually, like an extended family might. They did not worry about material possessions or their public image, and they trusted each other to do what was right for the others. The Bible shows us that these people were happy, sincere and appreciated by nonbelievers because of their integrated faith. Their love for Christ and awe at how God was working among them enabled them to introduce thousands of people to Christ every day. I am convinced that if the typical unchurched person were invited to get involved with such a collection of believers— people engaged in the kind of life described in these few verses—they would jump at the opportunity.

And why shouldn't everyone have the chance? God created us to be involved in such a church. Jesus died so that we might have the opportunity to share that kind of fellowship. The Holy Spirit was given to us so that we might foster such a dynamic and transforming vehicle for ministry. All of heaven is pulling for us to "do church" the way in which the Lord intended. Our hearts naturally yearn for such a spiritual family on Earth.

What, then, will it take for us to get from here to there? What will have to happen to move us to enfold America in God's designated entity for spiritual development and nurture?

I believe the answer relates to *commitment*. It will take a true commitment to God. It will take commitment to a vision of how each of us might truly be the Church, not just attend one. It will require a commitment to love and serve all people. It will take a commitment to use our gifts and resources to develop a living body of believers that is indistinguishable in essence from the Church described in Acts 2.

Are you willing to make such a commitment? This is not meant to be a rhetorical question. This is big—a big vision and a big promise. Let me explain what I think we will face when we say "yes" and make this pledge.

COMMITMENT TO GOD

According to *Merriam-Webster's New Collegiate Dictionary*, "commit" means "to put into charge or trust (entrust)" and "to pledge or assign to some particular course or use."[1]

> We take the first step toward truly preparing to reach the unchurched when we become models of faithfulness, obedience, holiness and righteousness.

When we commit ourselves to God, we entrust our lives to Him and pledge ourselves to the course He sets before us. Much of the pain and hardship we endure from day to day could be alleviated if we would truly devote ourselves to knowing, loving and serving God, and to living in the ways He prescribes in the Bible. The Scriptures, of course, caution us that we will never totally eliminate societal problems, such as poverty and hunger; nor will we escape the consequences of our humanity (emotional distress, physical pain, bad choices, etc.). However, when we commit our lives to God we, in essence, declare that we will trust Him in these matters.

It is amazing that two-thirds of all Americans think that the purpose of life is to enjoy blessings and gain the maximum fulfillment from their options and temptations. God's plan is clearly different. He hopes we will become single-minded about life, fully focused on Him. However, many of us have become distracted. In fact, the growth of the

American economy is largely based upon developing newer, bigger, better, more sophisticated distractions. He allows it, but He is not honored by it.

We take the first step toward truly preparing to reach the unchurched when we become living representations of His intended Church, models of faithfulness, obedience, holiness and righteousness. God's Church is not about structures, systems and resources; it is about individual people and our relationships with God. When those associations are in order, we will affect others around us, whether we want to or not.

The Power of Influence

One of the most impressive characteristics of well-known religious leaders is their ability to influence people who do not know them personally. Mother Teresa affected people that way. If you watched her, listened to her or read her teachings, her passion for God and her determination to live the way He called her to live probably moved you deeply. It caused some people to be excited about the possibilities; it created in some an internal guilt regarding the gap between them and God; it generated in others a desire to reflect more deeply on life's meaning and potential. Billy Graham has the same effect on people.

Have you ever encountered a person like that in your life? We love to be around people like this because they have something that is attractive, something that is different but compelling.

The key question is: As believers in Christ, why aren't we such models? This is what God had in mind for us.

As we ponder ways to approach the unchurched people we know, let's think about the nature of our own commitments to God. Our offer to the unchurched should not to be "Come join an organization" or "Come hang out with our nice group of people." The offer should be "You, too, can have a relationship with God that will restore in you the same thing that we experience and that we have become." Jesus expressed this when He said to His disciples, "Follow Me" (Matt. 19:21). What the unchurched must do is follow Jesus—completely, unashamedly, joyfully, willingly and longingly. If that is going to happen, we who already follow Jesus must show them the way.

Walk the Faith

If we are honest with ourselves, part of the reason why many people remain unchurched is that they have looked us over and do not especially like what they see. Some of us talk the faith but do not live it. Others do not even talk it very well.

Maybe we have never thought of ourselves as hypocrites, but how many of us would pass this test: How many people can you name who have reexamined their lives because there was something in your life that they saw and craved but did not possess? That something is more than just having said a prayer to determine salvation. It is a continual awareness of, and response to, the presence of God—a spiritual, emotional, intellectual and physical transformation that is accomplished by giving the Holy Spirit free rein and that results in an entirely new way of being God's Church on Earth.

> Many people remain unchurched because they have looked us over and do not especially like what they see.

The results of years of research is clear on this point: Many people name Jesus as their savior, but relatively few have lives that consistently demonstrate He is truly the Lord of their hearts, minds and souls. Perhaps before we invite other people to take part in the things of God, we should commit ourselves to experience fully all that is available to us through Jesus. When that happens, we will not have to worry too much about attracting and assimilating others into the Church. When God becomes the true priority in our lives, and when we imitate the heart of Christ and live in the power of the indwelling Spirit, what we represent will be irresistible.

Note

1. *Merriam-Webster's New Collegiate Dictionary*, 10th ed., s.v. "commit."

HOW MANY UNCHURCHED PEOPLE ARE THERE IN AMERICA?

A. Fewer than 5 million

B. 20 to 25 million

C. 50 to 55 million

D. 95 to 100 million

E. More than 125 million

F. Too many to count

CHAPTER 2 ─────

SIZING UP THE UNCHURCHED

Cross-cultural studies consistently demonstrate the religious bent of Americans. Compared to people of other countries, we are more likely to believe in God, pray, own Bibles, give money to religious organizations and attend church services. Ask people on the street about their religious convictions, and more than four out of five will describe themselves as Christians and most have some sense of the basic lessons and principles taught in the Bible—even though they may not believe them or live in accordance with them.

A CHRISTIAN NATION?

One of the enduring qualities that defines the nation today, as it did back in 1776, is an appreciation for religious freedom and involvement.

There is, however, a story within this story. Yes, most Americans call themselves Christians and most are willing to associate with some type of Christian church, usually Protestant or Roman Catholic. But the moral and philosophical ambiguities that have reshaped our culture in recent years have affected our religious perspectives and practices, too. Being a Christian has lost much of its meaning in this age of relativism, tolerance, diversity, ecumenism and syncretism. To say that Americans are a people of deep faith simply because of the breadth of our religious activity is about as intelligent as claiming that we are the healthiest people on Earth because we eat the most pounds of food per capita each year.

Consider, for instance, what people mean when they say they are "Christian." Overall, this term has become a generic description indicating that the individual believes in a universal deity (generally labeled "God") and would agree that there was a historical person known as Jesus Christ who was a great teacher and miracle worker. To be Christian in America indicates that you probably own a Bible, occasionally attend church services and believe that religious faith is at least somewhat important in your life. The significance of that faith is manifested by regular engagement with God through prayer, belief in the power of angels and the contention that involvement in some faith system is better than faith abstinence.

> Being a Christian has lost much of its meaning in this age of relativism, tolerance, diversity, ecumenism and syncretism.

A Born-Again Minority

While most Americans say they are Christians they do not necessarily mean that they have any type of vital relationship with Jesus Christ or that they believe that their eternal outcome depends on Him. A minority of people in America are born-again—meaning that they have an ongoing, personal relationship with God through Jesus Christ, that they have confessed their sins to God and that they believe they will live with God for eternity solely because of the grace extended to them through that relationship with Christ. The number of people in the United States who are *not* born-again Christians is about 180 to 190 million people.[1] If that group were a nation unto itself, it would be the fourth most populated nation on the planet, behind only China, India and Indonesia!

The Unchurched in America

There is another significant group that we must consider—the group that is the focus of this book. These are unchurched Americans—people who do not attend a Christian church, in spite of the presence of 324,000 Protestant and 20,000 Roman Catholic congregations throughout the nation. The unchurched population varies in size from year to year, but it generally encompasses about one-third of the adult population and slightly less among young people. In mid-2000, we at Barna

Research estimated that about 95 to 100 million Americans of all ages were unchurched.

We define a person as unchurched if he or she has not attended a Christian church service at any time during the past six months, other than special events such as weddings and funerals.

If all of the unchurched people in the United States were a nation of their own, they would be the eleventh most populated country on Earth. Only Bangladesh, Brazil, China, India, Indonesia, Japan, Mexico, Nigeria, Pakistan and Russia would have a greater head count. The unchurched equal triple the number of people who currently reside in California. It is like having 13 New York Cities—all five boroughs—combined.

Clearly, the religious nature of America has not affected the life of every person in the same way. And for nearly 100 million of our fellow citizens, the Church is not part of their lives. For those of us who are out-reach oriented—and that should include all who call Jesus their savior—reaching the unchurched with both the good news of the grace extended to them by Jesus and the benefit of being part of His Church is one of the greatest challenges we face in this life.

THE BIG PICTURE

Some of the facts and insights you read in this book will surprise you. Other chapters will confirm what you have experienced or suspected. To set the stage for a deeper discussion of the many insights we at Barna Research have gained into the minds and hearts of the unchurched, I will first summarize some of the important big-picture insights and then dissect them in greater detail in the chapters that follow.

An Increasing Interest in Spiritual Matters
In these first years of the new millennium and in the days following the terrorist attacks of September 11, 2001, there has been great interest in the Christian Church. Many individuals whose past affiliation with churches was only marginal or unfulfilling have sought a deeper

connection with their faith and have been open to the idea of participating in a community of faith. Many of them, however, have not known
where to start. They have been bewildered by the massive array of choices, and yet have been mostly ignorant of the full range and substance of
the options.

The Importance of Relationships

The unchurched cover the spectrum of people groups in society. A study
of the averages reveals that most of them are fairly typical of the aggregate population in terms of age, marital status and regional location.
However, the unchurched are more likely than the norm of the population to be male, to have experienced a divorce, to have more education,
and to have a larger income.

One of the important revelations in this research is that unchurched
people are not "people persons." They tend to be more combative, less
relational, lonelier and less flexible. They want a church that is a caring
community, but they are not especially willing to bend over backward to
fit the relational style they require of a congregation.

Do not assume that the unchurched feel they need God because they
are miserable. These are aggressive, energetic and driven people. They
have made something of themselves—at least by the world's standards.
Their hard-charging lifestyle has left many of them frazzled from stress
and broken relationships, but they do not necessarily believe that God,
Jesus, religion, the Bible, faith or Christianity will help them overcome
the struggles they face. They are open to the possibility, but not predis-
posed to believing that the answer will be based on a religious faith.

The reasons why these people avoid church can be viewed from two
different angles. On the one hand, we can point out that they do not
attend church largely because they do not think it is worth the time and
effort.

On the other hand, given the unchurched person's vulnerability to
expressions of faith, we also know that a huge explanation for their
absence from church is that they have not been invited to participate. The
chances of unchurched people coming to a worship service on their own,
without soft but continual encouragement from trusted friends, is slim.

Unchurched people are more likely to respond to a personal invitation than they are to surrender to pressure to belong to a group. They will be attracted via personal relationships more than media marketing. The approach must be personal, but not pushy, and entertaining, yet relevant and substantive. Expect the unchurched to resist highly-polished marketing efforts. They are skeptical of institutions, specifically of slick religiosity. The local church still needs to evince quality and conduct effective outreach, but it cannot fall prey to gimmickry.

Being Creative and Flexible in Outreach

There is not a one-size-fits-all strategy that will unlock the gates to reaching the unchurched. Like everything else in our world, attracting this population requires multiple strategies, coherent with each other, undertaken simultaneously. The most successful church marketing strategies, however, will be sensitive to the unchurched's needs for control, perceived value and a personal touch.

Just as political campaigns use imagery, symbols and terminology to reach the hearts of people, so must the faith community utilize such tools. Among the substantive hooks that will speak positively to the unchurched are the notions of compassion to others, applied faith principles, healthy families, love of children, genuine interpersonal caring, efficient use of time through the delivery of relevant substance, integrity, authenticity and personal experience.

> Unchurched people are more likely to respond to a personal invitation than they are to surrender to pressure to belong to a group.

The components of a dream church vary from one unchurched person to the next. In general, most will seek a group of 100 to 200 people, a casual atmosphere, a place that demonstrates reverence for God, the integration of meaningful traditions, practical and topical preaching and other individually customized features.

The unchurched are quite focused on the matters that they believe to be important. For example, God is vital, but the church is not.

Another example: Being a Christian matters, being born-again does not. Naturally, these perceptions can change, but be aware of what is most common.

Most unchurched people are open to becoming involved in church life, but they are not actively seeking such an association. They tend to be material first, spiritual second.

Rechurching the Born-Again Unchurched

A small *but significant* proportion of unchurched adults are born-again Christians—almost one out of five. Remember, the definition of an unchurched person is someone who has not been to church in the last six months except for special occasions. This includes some who are born-again. If church leaders understood these people better, this group would be a natural segment to attract back to the church.

Rechurching this group alone would swell Sunday morning attendance by more than 15 million people—which, if evenly distributed across the nation's 350,000 or so Christian churches, would equal more than 40 new people per congregation. That inflow would constitute the largest return to the Church during any decade in the past century and would increase the size of the average Protestant church by almost half!

Strategies That Work

Some forward-looking churches are experiencing tremendous success at relating to the unchurched. However, there is not a standard formula or program that works everywhere. Getting to know the unchurched at an intimate level and then designing relational strategies around their needs and aspirations appears to be one common element that makes a difference.

A DEEPER LOOK

Relational strategies are only the stepping-stone. Let's dive into the discoveries we have made from our research among the unchurched. By understanding this important group of people better, we can better serve their needs and honor God.

Do you want to see the lives of people changed by the power of God and converted into positive energy for the purposes of His kingdom? Are you looking for ways to minister with impact among a group of people who are spiritually confused and may not even realize it? Would you like to see attendance at Christian churches in America, including your home church, explode with new participants who are hungry for a taste of genuine truth and significance? Have you watched in dismay as the morals, values and lifestyles of our nation have decayed, and have you wondered what you could do to help bring about a moral and spiritual revolution that would improve our society and its peoples?

If you answered "yes" to any of these questions, then read on. God is calling you to represent Him in the lives of a nation within our nation: the unchurched of America.

Note
1. OmniPoll™ 1-02, January 2002 and YouthPoll™ 01, October 2001 (national surveys conducted by the Barna Research Group, Ltd., Ventura, CA).

WHAT DO UNCHURCHED ADULTS LIKE LEAST ABOUT THEIR PAST CHURCH EXPERIENCES?

A. strict and inflexible beliefs
B. hypocritical behavior of Christians
C. pressure to join the church
D. being told what to do or how to live
E. too much emphasis on giving money
F. the worship services are too long

CHAPTER 3

WHY PEOPLE AVOID CHURCH

On the face of it, given who the typical unchurched person is, staying disconnected from church makes no sense. Most unchurched people think of themselves as Christians. Most of them own Bibles—the very book that describes the importance of being connected to God's chosen ones in a true community of faith. Among the greatest needs of Americans today are to become relationally attached to other people, to find the answers to life's big questions and to make a difference in the world—all lifelong quests that the Church exists to facilitate. One of the foremost concerns among American adults is the deterioration of moral values in our nation, an issue of paramount concern within Christian congregations. And one of the primary desires held by millions of people is that their children be able to have a well-rounded, positive and moral education. It would seem to be a natural choice for people to turn to the Church to meet each of these longings.

Yet nearly 100 million people live without a connection to a faith-based community. Activating and guiding those people in spiritual matters is one of the daunting challenges of our age. It is a God-sized task that demands tremendous faith, courage and determination—and reliance upon His Holy Spirit for the wisdom and tools to get the job done.

Undoubtedly, the first step in the process of making a connection with the unchurched is to pray for the tools and the opportunities to influence those lives for Christ. A reasonable second step would be to figure out why such massive numbers of people avoid a connection with a church.

Let's be clear from the start: About half of all unchurched adults were formerly churched people. There are two interesting facets to this observation.

First, when Barna Research conducted similar studies 15 years ago, we found that the number of unchurched adults who had previously been churched was much higher than it is today. In the mid-1980s, about four out of every five unchurched adults had at one time been churched. This radical shift is largely a consequence of the fact that a large proportion of Baby-Boomer parents broke with tradition and did not regularly bring their kids to church. Many of the Boomers who did give their kids exposure to church life did so inconsistently. The consequence is a large portion of people within the Baby-Bust generation who completely or mostly lack church experience.

The second important facet is that half of all unchurched adults have made a conscious decision to drop out from church life. Reconnecting those people with a local church will typically require us to address their past experiences first, before we can attempt to get them to consider reengagement seriously.

REASONS FOR DROPPING OUT

There are several ways to gain insight into the reasons behind the exodus and absence of the unchurched. We can ask them what they liked least about their church experiences, assuming that their disappointments and frustrations drove their choice to leave and avoid the church now. Alternatively, we can ask them why they have decided not to attend a Christian church. We have asked both of these questions and received answers that were similar, but with some important nuances to consider.

To the question about what they did not like about their past church experiences, there were three common answers. The first was that they disliked the hypocritical behavior of church people. "They get all pious and religious on Sunday morning, but they forget about their religion the rest of the week" was a representative assessment provided to us by one of the unchurched women we interviewed. The alleged hypocrisy of church attendees was especially bothersome to people in their 50s and beyond, as well as among divorced adults. About one out of every five unchurched adults found this contradictory behavior problematic (see table 3.1).

A second aspect that many of the unchurched deemed repulsive was the strict and inflexible beliefs of the church. "They tell you what you're supposed to believe—they do not leave any room for discussion or interpretation," explained one disenchanted former church regular. The types of people most upset about the theological rigidity of churches tend to be those who earn above-average incomes and residents of the Western states. Again, one out of five people listed this as a reason for their failure to make church a part of their weekly regimen.

The third common answer, also given by one-fifth of the unchurched, is that there is nothing in particular that they disliked about the church. To these people, the church was simply not compelling. "Look, if you want my time and energy, no problem—as long as you deliver the goods," warned an unchurched Boomer from Missouri. "I went to a church for years, but never got much out of it. After a while you figure there's not much to be gained by that affiliation. I hate wasting my time; there's too much to experience in life. So I've moved on."

Naturally, other reasons were given, too. One out of every eight people said they did not like the way the church worshiped. One out of every ten felt the church was too focused on raising money. Smaller numbers of people listed reasons such as the feeling of superiority conveyed by the congregation, the pressure to join or to return, and being told how to live.

Table 3.1
What Unchurched Adults Liked Least About Their Past Church Experiences
(Number in survey: 230)

Hypocritical behavior of the churched	21%
Strict/inflexible beliefs	21
Nothing in particular	21
The worship service (long, boring, etc.)	12
Too much emphasis on giving money	9
Air of superiority among the churched	6
Pressure to join/return to the church	4
They tell you what to do/how to live	4

Too Busy for Church

When we asked unchurched adults to describe why they currently do not attend a church, the top-rated reasons were that they were too busy to do so (or had scheduling conflicts), that the church had nothing of interest to offer and that the individual was just not interested in being involved in a church. These reasons describe the reticence of almost half of the unchurched. The life stages of the respondents were clearly related to their answers. For instance, parents of kids under 18 were the most likely to say they were too busy for church. Senior citizens and those with college degrees were the most likely to say that the church has nothing of value to offer them (see table 3.2).

Different Religious Beliefs

A sizeable segment (one-seventh) responded that their religious beliefs differ significantly from those of the church crowd. This was most common among Baby Busters (people under 37) and among wealthy adults (people who earn $75,000 per year or more and those with a college degree).

These particular protestations are not surprising. Busters, many of whom possess postmodern perspectives and others of whom have crafted unique theological views, are notably sensitive to belonging to groups that demonstrate ideological tolerance and embrace the notion of diversity. In fact, a recent study we conducted among teenagers showed that young people increasingly feel comfortable with substantive contradictions while they feel limited by rigidly consistent frames of thought. Meanwhile, wealthy individuals tend to be less concerned about tolerance but are quite confident in their own intellectual abilities and conclusions. A blanket acceptance of the party line, no matter who the party is, often does not sit well with these individuals.

No Need for Church

About one out of every eight unchurched people write off the church because they do not believe in organized religion or in the necessity of worshiping God through a church experience.

Many Other Reasons

Each of the remaining reasons represents a relatively small segment of the unchurched population. For instance, only 4 percent say the beliefs of churches are too rigid or inflexible. Three percent mentioned that they dislike church people or that the church is only interested in their money. Each of the following reasons was named by 2 percent: they do not believe in God or Jesus; they had bad past experiences in church; a physical disability precludes their attendance; they have not found a church they like; they are held up by family issues; and they are not religious or Christian.

Do not overlook the fact that 15 percent say they do not attend church but they do not know why. Qualitative research we have conducted in the past has shown that most of those people, when pressed, simply have little interest in a church or have not felt a need to get involved in one.

Did you notice the extraordinarily small numbers of people who avoid church because they do not believe in God or in Jesus? Or the small number who contend that the church is too money-hungry to justify their presence? Or the relative handful who have been chased away by bad past experiences? How affirming and encouraging it is to find that people tend not to avoid the church for "irreconcilable differences"!

> **M**illions of the unchurched do not care about church involvement because they do not see any need to get involved.

OVERCOMING THE BARRIERS

What are the obstacles we must overcome? The major considerations are indifference and value. Millions of the unchurched do not care about church involvement because they do not see any need to get involved. Millions more stay away because they cannot make the value equation work. In other words, when they calculate the amount of time, money and energy they would have to invest in church, they do not see a reasonable return on the investment. Unchurched people, like most Americans, are practical individuals. They do not get excited by promises perceived to be unrealistic, such as "This church will change your life," or "You will never feel more loved than when you become part of this fellowship"; nor are they swayed by extensive religious programs. They want personal benefits that they understand and desire. Most of the unchurched figure they have gotten along just fine without a church for a long time, and until someone gives them reason to feel otherwise, they will remain spiritually unattached.

Table 3.2
The Main Reasons Why People Do Not Currently Attend a Church

Main reason for not attending church	2000	1990
No time; schedule conflicts; working	26%	24%
Not interested; nothing to offer; no reason	16	16
My beliefs are different than the church's	14	9
Don't believe in organized religion/ don't need to worship at a church	12	8
Their beliefs are too rigid/too inflexible	4	*
Dislike the church people; they're hypocrites	3	2
The church only wants my money	3	2
Don't believe in God/Jesus	2	2
Had bad experiences at church in the past	2	2
Physical disabilities prevent going	2	*
Haven't found a church I like	2	*
Family considerations/disagreements	2	1
I am not Christian/not religious	2	*
Dislike denominations/denom. churches	*	6
Churches are irrelevant to my life	1	5
Other	5	5
Don't know	15	22
Sample size	831	406

(* indicates less than one-half of 1 percent)

A DECADE OF CHANGE

Take another look at the data in table 3.2. The table contains not only the reasons why the unchurched stayed out of church in 2000, but also the reasons that were given by the unchurched in 1990. What changes took place in the intervening 10 years?

Very few, it seems. The main reasons why people fail to go to church stayed the same, as did the proportions of people who listed each of those reasons. In fact, the two lists bear a striking similarity from top to bottom. You might conclude that the psychological obstacles to reaching the unchurched have changed little in the last decade.

There are, however, a few minor shifts that reveal an important pattern. Notice that three of the four most commonly cited reasons for remaining unchurched (different beliefs, doctrinal rigidity and don't believe in organized religion) were more likely to be offered in 2000 than in 1990. The thread that ties those three items together is that they all relate to the penchant for personal expression, independent thinking and the adoption of diversity and tolerance as a philosophical mantra. With postmodernism and even nihilism becoming more prevalent in our culture, the trend toward rejecting absolutes and uncompromised principles continues to gather steam. Here, again, is a contradiction: Unchurched people desire experiences that are substantive, helpful and efficient, yet they reject the foundations of one of the world's most proven, time-tested solutions to their needs simply because it seems inflexible and unyielding.

The decline in the percentage of adults who do not know why they avoid church is also noteworthy. As noted earlier, although many of those who cannot articulate why they remain distant from church are actually indicating that it has failed to provide them with sufficient value, the decline in the "don't know" response is partly a reflection of people taking the Church more seriously as a lifestyle option these days. A decade or two ago, most unchurched people had pretty much made up their mind that church was not in their future plans—end of story. Today, however, with the moral chaos, loss of personal vision, search for meaning and pop culture fascination with spirituality, the church is not as easily dismissed as a viable alternative. Many adults who are presently unchurched arrived at that state after serious consideration of the value of church. Their conclusion—"no, but thank you"—does not minimize the fact that they were (and that many remain) willing to consider personal involvement in a local faith community.

WALKING A FINE LINE

One creed of the unchurched must be the well-worn Clint Eastwood line: "Make my day." If that day is to be Sunday, you make it worthwhile for these outsiders by providing perceived and delivered value. What you provide may well have to be a multifaceted value product: part spiritual, part relational, part practical and part entertainment. Because so many of the unchurched are not born-again, and therefore have no real relationship with Jesus, attracting and retaining these people will take more than a good worship service, since the very practice of worship is outside of their frame of comprehension and experience. They need a solid worship experience.

To provide what the unchurched seek will require us to walk a fine line between what they want and what we can provide without losing our character. For instance, we must walk the fine line between providing them personal benefits without compromising biblical truths and traditions. We must walk the fine line between giving them what they deem to be of value but without promising more than we can realistically deliver or delivering less than we can theologically justify. We must walk the fine line between being open, loving and accepting, and remaining true to our spiritual convictions.

Keep in mind that attracting the unchurched is not solely about marketing. Take another look at the reasons why people do not go to church and why they left church in the first place. No amount of clever marketing will overcome boring, irrelevant or seemingly endless worship services.

While you're examining the tables that describe what they do not want to experience in a church, read between the lines. Clearly, they are not looking for an institutional attachment. Translation: They are not looking for an organization or group to join. Even the Busters and

Mosaics, our two youngest and most relational generations, are not seeking the church as a social vehicle. Also, the unchurched are not quietly asking for a guilt trip related to their rejection of God, His people or His events. Making them feel bad for shirking God and providing a pat solution (i.e., "Come join us as we gather together to celebrate our relationship with Him.") will do more harm than good.

A final word of caution is in order regarding the implementation of whatever strategy you deploy for reaching the unchurched. The data tell us that the reasons why they stay away don't change much over time. We're in the midst of the fastest moving period in American history, a time when our society reinvents itself two or three times a decade—yet, the reasons why the unchurched reject the church remained consistent in the last 10 years (at least). If you develop a viable plan for reaching and connecting with the unchurched, and it doesn't all fall into place as quickly as you had hoped, don't rush to scrap the plan and start over. Give your well-conceived strategy time to work its magic. Better yet, give the Holy Spirit time to work through you and your people in your honest efforts to build relational bridges to the unchurched. Time is of the essence, but frantic and constant revising of sound strategy is foolish. Get a strategy you're comfortable with, undergird it with prayer and superb follow-through, and trust God for the results.

AT WHAT AGE IS A PERSON MOST LIKELY TO RECEIVE CHRIST AS SAVIOR?

A. 5 to 13
B. 14 to 18
C. 19 to 25
D. 26 to 40
E. 41 to 60
F. 61 and over

CHAPTER 4

A DEMOGRAPHIC PROFILE OF THE UNCHURCHED

We use demographic information all the time. When we interact with a person in their 70s, we probably do not bother to talk about the latest rock music or *VeggieTales* videos because we know neither is relevant to them. When we go out to lunch with a college student, we probably do not wait for them to pick up the check because we know that their budget is limited. When we visit friends in California, we are likely to avoid talking about hurricanes, since they do not have them; but we might discuss earthquakes.

All of these choices we make are predicated on demographic knowledge. Demographic characteristics are common background traits, such as a person's gender, age, income, education, region of residence and racial heritage. Because such attributes are based upon stable conditions (i.e., we cannot change our ethnicity, and our age progresses in a very predictable manner) rather than variable conditions (e.g., our attitudes about life or our hopes for the future), demographics become a very useful tool for understanding today's conditions and predicting tomorrow's probabilities. But as we intuitively realize, those traits may also enable us to have greater impact upon a person or group.

For example, we know that people who make more than $100,000 annually are less receptive to potluck dinners or home visitation than are middle-class or working-class people (although nobody is terribly excited about either of those strategies any more). We know that women are more interested in relationships and in ministries that connect people than are men. We know that Baby Busters are the generation most likely to reject sermons that tell them what to do. They prefer stories and questions that challenge what and how they think, and they want such information offered in a nonjudgmental manner. These are just a few examples of demographic insights that can be translated into effective ministry strategies.

There are exceptions to every rule, of course, but when you strive to craft a strategy or plan for effective ministry, those approaches will be most effective if based upon knowledge and facts about the people whose lives you wish to impact. Demographic information is not the only body of knowledge that should be integrated into your strategies, but it is certainly a helpful building block. With that in mind, let's examine the demographic background of the unchurched.

MEN AND WOMEN

Men constitute slightly less than half of the national population, but they represent a slight majority of the unchurched (54 percent) (see table 4.1). Since 1990, in spite of the efforts of various ministries aimed at men, the male proportion of the unchurched has increased. (Imagine what the numbers might be if we had not focused on awakening the hearts of men.)

Table 4.1
The Demographic Profile of the Unchurched and Churched Populations

	(N = 1507)	(N = 1336)
	Unchurched	**Churched**
Gender:		
Male	54%	46%
Female	46	54

Continued on next page

	(N = 1507) **Unchurched**	(N = 1336) **Churched**
How many fit this age range?		
18 to 24 years old	15%	11%
25 to 34	19	17
35 to 49	35	33
50 to 64	20	23
65 or older	11	16
How many achieved these educational levels?		
High school graduate, or less	46%	46%
Some college, did not graduate	26	26
College graduate	28	28
Household income, before taxes:		
Under $20,000	19%	13%
$20,000 to $39,999	36	39
$40,000 to $74,999	26	30
$75,000 or more	18	18
How many fit these marital segments?		
Currently married	53%	57%
Have never been married	26	22
Currently divorced	13	12
Currently separated	2	2
Widowed	6	8
Have ever been divorced	31	23
Racial heritage:		
White/Caucasian	74%	70%
Black/African-American	8	14
Hispanic	11	12
Asian-American	3	4
Other	3	1

Continued on next page

	(N = 1507) Unchurched	(N = 1336) Churched
Have kids under 18 living in household		
	36%	32%
Region:		
Northeast	27%	19%
Midwest	20	24
South	27	37
West	26	20
Medians:		
Age	41 years	44 years
Years of education	14 years	13 years
Household income (pre-tax)	$36,697	$39,245

We can observe the data in table 4.1 from a different angle to gain even greater perspective on this. Overall, almost 4 out of every 10 men stay away from church, compared to about three out of every 10 women. That may not seem like a big difference, but when you project it over the aggregate populations of each of these groups, the gap becomes enormous. If we assume that there are about 70 million unchurched adults, then we estimate that roughly 38 million of them are men and about 32 million are women. That gap of 6 million people is equivalent to the entire population of Massachusetts or Indiana.

> In spite of ministry efforts aimed at men, the male proportion of the unchurched has increased.

In comparing unchurched men and women, we also discovered that men were much more likely than women never to have been married; were much more likely to reside in the South; and that there were twice as many nonwhite unchurched men as there were nonwhite unchurched women. Unchurched men were also considerably less likely than women not to be registered to vote. This is significant because it typically reflects people who are less engaged in society and relationships.

THE YOUNG AND CHURCHLESS

While young adults have a reputation for comprising a disproportion-ately large share of the unchurched, that bad rap is somewhat mislead-ing. It is true that they are more broadly represented than their share of the general population warrants—but not by as much as has been sug-gested. Adults between the ages of 18 and 34—in essence, the Baby Busters—make up one-third of the unchurched, but slightly more than one-fourth of the churched base. At the other end of the spectrum are adults 50 and older, who represent almost 4 out of every 10 churched adults and comprise just 3 out of 10 unchurched people.

The median age of the two segments shows the difference between these groups from a different angle. The median age of the churched is 44; that of the unchurched is 41. A gap of that magnitude is noticeable and sta-tistically significant, but hardly monumental. (For instance, the median age of people who buy rap music is under 30; the median age of those who buy classical is over 50. That is a gap that you can do something with!)

The median age of the unchurched has risen significantly during the past decade, from 35 years of age in 1990 to the current level. This indi-cates that as the unchurched segment continues to change, it is both keeping its base as they age and attracting an increasing share of people over 45—especially among the two older generations (Builders and Seniors). In 10 years the proportion of people 50 and older who are unchurched jumped from 22 percent to 31 percent. That rise compen-sated for the decline in the share of church absentees under 35, plum-meting from 47 percent to just 34 percent.

THE EDUCATION SCORE

About half of the unchurched have gone as far as completing high school, one-fourth have attended college without graduating, and the remaining one-quarter graduated from college. The educational achieve-ment profile of the churched population is identical.

THE MONEY FACTOR

The close tie between education and income, combined with the revelation that the churched and unchurched have virtually identical records of educational achievement, would lead us to expect the two groups to have similar household income levels. Such is not the case, however. Based on median household income levels, the churched earn about 7 percent more income than unchurched adults. This is not attributable to differences in educational achievement, but it may be a consequence of the older average age of the churched.

What makes this small gap more significant is that the general demographic nature of the unchurched would lead us to expect the unchurched to have the higher average income. The larger shares of unchurched emanating from the Northeast and West, the higher proportion of men and the higher percentage of whites—all of which are groups whose median income exceeds the national norm—would support such an expectation. But this is why we do research: to discover things that we did not know or did not expect, and to figure out what it means and what to do about it.

FAMILY SITUATIONS

The marital status of the two target groups is quite similar. Slightly more than half of each group is currently married (53 percent among the unchurched, 57 percent among the churched) and about one-quarter of each segment is made up of people who have never been married (26 percent and 22 percent, respectively). The remaining one-quarter is divided between those who are divorced (about 1 out of 8), widowed (1 out of every 16) and those who are presently separated from their spouse (1 out of every 50).

In 1990, slightly less than half of all unchurched adults were married; a decade later, slightly more than half were married. The percentage of unchurched adults who have never been married dropped from 32 percent in 1990 to 26 percent in 2000. Even so, the chances of being unchurched are much higher if a person has never walked the aisle.

Among adults who have never been married, close to half (44 percent) are unchurched—significantly higher than the chance of a married adult being unchurched (29 percent).

In terms of the total number of people, there are more unchurched people who are married than unchurched people who are single but only because there are more married adults than there are single adults.

We also found that about one-third of all unchurched households contain children under the age of 18. If we explore the aggregate number of unchurched children (under 18) in America, we estimate that figure to be in the range of 25 to 30 million individuals. Keep in mind that the youth segment is especially important when we talk about spiritual impact. A study we conducted recently revealed that if we calculate the probabilities of people accepting Jesus Christ as their savior, those between the ages of 5 and 13 have a 32 percent probability; individuals in the 14 to 18 age range have a 4 percent probability; and people between the ages of 19 and death have a 6 percent chance. In other words, we have the greatest window of opportunity for reaching people with the gospel before they reach their teenage years. The chances of seeing their spiritual life change after that point are relatively slim.

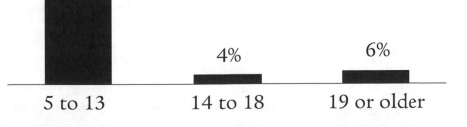

PROBABILITY OF ACCEPTING CHRIST AS SAVIOR

32%

4%

6%

5 to 13   14 to 18   19 or older

EFFECTS OF ETHNICITY

Abstaining from church life is less palatable to African-Americans than to other ethnic segments of America. Consider this: Blacks constitute 14 percent of the Church population and just 8 percent of the unchurched population. This is because fewer than one out of every four black adults avoid church. By contrast, slightly more than one-third of all white and Hispanic adults remain unattached to a church. A majority of Hispanics remains affiliated with Roman Catholic churches—the only ethnic group in America of which a majority embrace Catholicism.

> Abstaining from church life is less palatable to African-Americans than to other ethnic segments of America.

REGIONAL DIFFERENCES

The trends regarding geography are not surprising. The two regions that supply a disproportionate share of the unchurched are the Northeast and West. Those two regions together represent 43 percent of the nation's population, 39 percent of the churched and 53 percent of the unchurched. By contrast, the residents of the South constitute 34 percent of America's total population, but they contribute 27 percent of the unchurched and 37 percent of the churched.

Given this, it is not surprising to learn that it is a lot easier to find unchurched folks along the coasts. In the Northeast (Maine through Washington, D.C.), 42 percent of all adults are unchurched. In the Western and mountain states, 39 percent of the resident adults have no church involvement. Those numbers are considerably higher than the parallel figures for the South (27 percent) and Midwest (30 percent).

THE NUMBERS IN PERSPECTIVE

Are you lost in the numbers? Let me free you from the tyranny of statistics. Memorizing or even understanding any of those numbers will do you relatively little good. There is value to be gained from such demographic discovery, but it must be put in perspective. Here is a outlook that might be helpful to you.

First, keep in mind that the profile of the unchurched demonstrates that there is tremendous diversity among these people. There are many different types of unchurched individuals, and each one of them matters to God. Keep in mind that even the smallest demographic niche identified in table 4.1—for instance, Asians, who are only 3 percent of the unchurched—represents a huge number of people. (There are more than 2 million unchurched Asian-American adults, plus another million or so children.) Unchurched people are not all the same.

Second, the demographic diversity of the unchurched requires that we develop a wide variety of informed and intentional strategies for reaching them. This is not a one-size-fits-all group of people. We must wisely and purposefully target different groups through different forms of ministry. Penetrating the unchurched world requires us to be creative and savvy. Good intentions alone will not get us too far.

Third, the changes witnessed over time suggest that some formerly churched people become unchurched while some unchurched people join the churched mass. This is to be expected in a fast-paced, change-oriented, highly mobile society. Yet, in spite of these fluctuations among the unchurched, the most significant fact is that the demographic character of the unchurched remains relatively stable over time. This consistency permits us the luxury of creating long-term approaches to winning back the unchurched.

Finally, notice that the unchurched are generally similar in background to the churched. However, we know that their *relationship* to the church is completely different. This suggests that demographic information may offer some helpful bits of wisdom, but that demographics alone are probably not the key to reaching the unchurched. You may expect to learn some valuable lessons about those who reject the Church, but the core revelations about what it will take to turn them into committed, growing and productive followers of Jesus Christ are to be found elsewhere.

With that in mind, let's consider some other dimensions of these people: their values, attitudes and lifestyles.

Table 4.2

The Percentage of Various Subgroups That Are Unchurched

Population subgroup	% who are Unchurched	Population subgroup	% who are Unchurched
AGE:		**GENDER:**	
18-24	46%	male	39%
25-34	36	female	28
35-49	33		
50-64	29	**ETHNICITY:**	
65 or older	23	white	34%
		black	23
EDUCATION:		Hispanic	34
high school or less	36%		
some college/trade			
school	32	**HOUSEHOLD INCOME**	
college graduate	32	**(PRE-TAX):**	
graduate studies	31	under $20,000	42%
		$20,000-$39,999	34
		$40,000-$74,999	28
MARITAL STATUS:		$75,000 or more	33
currently married	29%		
never been married	44	**REGION:**	
separated	36	Northeast	42%
divorced	34	Midwest	30
widowed	26	South	27
		West	39
HAVE KIDS UNDER 18 AT HOME:			
yes	24%		
no	35		

WHICH OF THE FOLLOWING DESCRIPTIONS IS MORE LIKELY TO BE ADOPTED BY AN UNCHURCHED PERSON THAN BY A CHURCHED PERSON?

A. enjoys deep discussion
B. is self-sufficient
C. avoids conflict whenever possible
D. is stressed out
E. is often misunderstood by others
F. likes to try new experiences

CHAPTER 5

VALUES, ATTITUDES AND LIFESTYLES

If we want to build bridges to the unchurched, we have to understand who they are. Knowing their demographic background is of some help, but we need to comprehend something more intimate about what makes them tick—we need to understand their spin on life. In this chapter, let's get closer to the heartbeat of the unchurched and examine how they view their own personality types, political leanings, interests and lifestyle choices.

HOW THEY SEE THEMSELVES

Psychologists and cultural analysts sometimes criticize surveys that ask people to describe themselves because, they point out, people often have a very skewed self-perception. The criticism is valid. We all see ourselves differently from the way others see us, partly because we have a distinct understanding of what we think and why we do certain things, and partly because other people observe us only in certain situations and for limited amounts of time.

Despite this shortcoming, delving into people's self-perceptions gives us a valuable entry into their lives. If we know how they see themselves, then we can better estimate what types of response they will have to various opportunities and challenges. Such insights make it easier for us to develop authentic relationships with them, to understand their responses to the world and to provide ministry that meets real needs and issues in their lives.

Similarities Between the Unchurched and the Churched

The data in table 5.1 reveals three things. First, for the most part, the unchurched and the churched describe themselves in the same way. Second, there are relatively few extreme answers, which means that there is great diversity within the body of unchurched adults. Third, the unchurched portray themselves as aggressive, controlling individuals—again, not unlike most other people—but an important trait to keep in mind.

Table 5.1
How the Unchurched Describe Themselves

	unchurched	churched
self-sufficient	94%	91%
like to try new experiences	81	76
like to keep things light	70	74
like to be in control of things	70	64
enjoy deep discussions	68	77
skeptical	62	57
avoid conflict whenever possible	60	74
financially comfortable	57	66
trying to find a few good friends	55	47
too busy	52	47
enjoy making tough decisions	51	53
searching for meaning and purpose	50	48
often misunderstood by others	44	32
in debt	42	38
stressed out	36	27
career comes first	33	16
dealing with an addiction	10	10
sample size	600	1402

Note that most unchurched people perceive themselves as self-sufficient, experimental and controlling. Relate that to what we seek to do in our churches and the kind of individuals we hope people will become (i.e., reliant upon God and controlled by the Spirit), and you can immediately see why so many of the unchurched have no interest in church involvement. As self-sufficient beings, they feel no compelling need to rely upon God for much of anything. As experimental individuals, they may well be turned off by the restrictions that Scripture and Church doctrine place on various lifestyles, entertainment forms and relationships. The urge to be in control is difficult to satisfy in a church, either theologically (God is in control) or operationally (the system is in place and is hard to change—just ask church leaders). In fact, exerting control over your church experience is particularly difficult when you are an outsider coming in to a church. The prevailing wisdom among the faithful is that the church exists to change that person, not to be changed by the newcomer.

There are a few distinctions between the two groups that are worthy of comment. Notice that the unchurched are distinguished by being less likely to avoid conflict and are more likely to feel financially comfortable. In contrast to the churched, they are more likely to feel misunderstood, to lack good friends, to feel stressed out and to place their career above all else. These traits do not describe all of the unchurched, but they begin to convey the impression that a sizeable number of unchurched peo-ple—at least by comparison to the churched—are driven, tough, perhaps even lonely individuals.

> **M**any of the unchurched appear to be frustrated, as indicated by their high levels of stress.

Many of the unchurched appear to be frustrated, as indicated by their high levels of stress, their confusion over meaning and purpose and their admission that their lives are just too busy. This irritation may also be fueled by the sense that in comparison to other people they are not getting ahead in life.

The Unchurched and Spirituality

Now look at the figures displayed in table 5.2. These figures reveal a lit-tle bit about how the unchurched think of themselves in spiritual terms. The highest-ranked self-defining term was "theologically liberal," an expression that makes most Protestant pastors turn pale. Nevertheless, almost half of the unchurched describe themselves this way, as do one-third of church attendees. By contrast, only 13 percent of pastors consider themselves theologically liberal.

Almost as many unchurched people labeled themselves theologically conservative (43 percent) as labeled themselves theologically liberal (46 percent). This is substantially different from the self-perceptions of the churched, among whom 6 out of 10 claimed to be theologically conservative and just 1 out of 3 said they were theologically liberal. The gap was even bigger with regard to Protestant pastors: 8 out of 10 pastors said they were theologically conservative and just 1 out of 8 embraced the label "theologically liberal."

Table 5.2
Spiritual Self-Descriptions

	unchurched	churched	Protestant senior pastors
theologically liberal	46%	32%	13%
theologically conservative	43	58	79
a committed Christian	39	87	N/A
deeply spiritual	37	71	N/A
charismatic or Pentecostal	21	21	29
an evangelical Christian	12	51	83
sample size	600	1402	601

Not surprisingly, the unchurched were only half as likely as the churched to describe themselves as committed Christians and deeply spiritual. They were only one-quarter as likely to say they are evangelical Christians. The shocker was that both the churched and unchurched were equally likely to brand themselves as charismatic or Pentecostal Christians.

This data fills in the portrait a bit more. Now we can see that although the unchurched may think of themselves as religious people, most of them do not believe that they are deeply spiritual or that their ties to Christianity are anything more than nominal. A Christian church or group of people, therefore, is nothing special to them; it is one option on the religious horizon but not necessarily a compelling alternative or even their first choice for spiritual enrichment.

The Unchurched and Life's Issues

Let's continue to piece the puzzle together by examining the figures in table 5.3. From this we learn even more about how the unchurched handle life. Again, three overarching insights emerge. First, their personality profile is incredibly similar to that of the churched. Second, in comparison to the churched, America's unchurched adults appear to be less relationally inclined—just as the data in previous chapters indicated. Third, most of these people see themselves as competent, pragmatic and capable of successfully interacting with people. They believe that their decision-making is more likely to be influenced by logic than emotion, but they perceive their choices to represent a good balance of the two inputs.

Unchurched Personality Types

Finally, consider the information provided in table 5.4. This data is related to the personal style profiles originally developed by Carlson Learning Systems, which developed a self-administered test known as the Performax (or DiSC) profile. This test examines how a person relates to the expectations of others and to pressure, and provides an index of behavior. No particular behavioral type is better than any other. The tool simply describes how a person handles reality. There are many variations on this approach that have been developed over the years, including the one we used in our surveys at Barna Research.

The information regarding the unchurched shows us that they are fairly evenly divided among the four profile types. One-quarter of them see themselves as directive, dominating individuals who love to take risks and make things happen. They thrive on problems and challenges and excel as catalysts of creative solutions and productive activity. These people are the doers of society, people who set out to accomplish great things. For a church to appeal to them, they are likely to require challenging tasks, a viable means of connecting with a group of believers (since connecting is neither their natural tendency nor a strength) and a good sense of the benefits and parameters of the Christian life. They may chaff at or even resent a laid-back ministry, since they are usually operating at full throttle. In fact, their aggressive approach to life and their failure to check the facts and build relationships before setting off to achieve something significant may rankle people—especially in the typically staid, predictable and high-control church world.

More than one-quarter of the unchurched are highly personable and energetic people. These are the classic extroverts who make life up as they go along and who motivate others through their upbeat personalities. Enthusiastic and entertaining, these people love to be the center of attention and to get everyone involved in activities. They disdain control and details, and they work on raw energy and intuition.

About one-quarter of the unchurched are stabilizing forces who pursue consistency, unity and continuity in their environments. These people are not pushy; rather, compliance is one of their strengths. They strive for cooperation and serenity in their environments, and they thrive on repetition and minimal change. These people are sometimes deemed "plodders," since they are reliable but slow-paced and resistant to innovation or creative ideas that intrude on what is known and comfortable.

One out of every five unchurched adults is a cautious individual, driven to attend to details and to be accurate. They rely on facts and work within parameters (e.g., laws, routines and instructions), and they keep things orderly and on track. They eschew risks and reserve judgment on issues until they have reliable information upon which to base their decisions. Their need for precision makes them seem overly critical; their need for planning and strategic thinking robs them of the joys that may emerge from spontaneity. They are suspect of quick decisions, do not trust others to do things right (and therefore are not good at delegating tasks to others) and are poor at finding compromises or diplomatic solutions.

Table 5.3
Personality Factors of the Unchurched and Churched

	unchurched	churched
practical and sensible	90%	95%
logical and analytical	84	82
usually focused on the details	82	80
comfortable with big ideas	79	73
a real "people-person"	79	89
sensitive or highly emotional	62	56
highly creative	55	57
make decisions based on feelings	55	56
searching for meaning in life	45	42
not well-organized	31	28
shy or introverted	28	24

Table 5.4
Personal Styles of the Unchurched

	unchurched	churched	Bible figures who exemplify this
Dominance	25%	16%	Joshua, Paul, Solomon, Stephen
Interaction	27	32	Barnabas, Saul, Peter, David
Steadiness	21	25	Isaac, Abraham, Jonathan, Ruth
Cautiousness	20	21	Luke, Moses, Noah, Thomas

- Dominance: risk-taker, determined, decision maker, competitive, problem solver, productive, enjoys challenges and is goal driven;
- Interaction: energetic, very verbal, spontaneous, friendly, optimistic, thinks out loud, popular and motivates others;
- Steadiness: loyal, avoids confrontation, dislikes change, patient, sympathetic, indecisive, sensitive and not demanding of others;
- Cautiousness: accurate, practical, reserved, orderly, factual, likes instructions, detailed and conscientious.

Note that unchurched adults are much more likely than churched adults to be in the dominating group. Unchurched adults are also somewhat less likely to be among the highly interactive, spontaneous people and are slightly less likely to be numbered among those who establish a steadying and stabilizing influence.

The Diversity of the Unchurched
Does it make sense that the same type of church experience is going to satisfy the intellectual, emotional and spiritual needs of such diverse groups of people? Our past research has shown that Christian congregations usually include a mixture of the four types, but that the predominant flavor or style of the church tends to attract a certain type of person more easily than others. Similarly, certain types of people have a greater impact on each of these groups—differing from group to group—and the church ministries to which a visitor is exposed may have varying degrees of appeal, based upon the unchurched person's personal profile.

This information alone makes clear the challenge inherent in attracting, retaining and assisting in the development of unchurched people. There are dozens of dynamics brewing beneath the surface that make penetrating their ranks so much more difficult than merely providing good music, comfortable seating and a stimulating sermon. For instance, there are lifestyle issues.

How They See Their Lifestyles

The overall pattern we have witnessed in our research is that the unchurched tend to be less engaged with the world than are churched adults. For example, they are more than 50 percent less likely to volunteer their time to help nonprofit organizations; they are 17 percent less likely to interact in a discussion with friends on moral or ethical issues during a typical week; they are 14 percent less likely to be registered to vote; they are less likely to support nonprofit organizations financially; and among the people who donate, the unchurched give to fewer organizations.

Politically, the unchurched are less likely to be registered as Republicans and more likely to be registered as Independents. Along the same lines, we found that they are twice as likely as the churched to describe themselves as "mostly liberal" on political and social issues and only half as likely to say they are "mostly conservative" on such matters.

> The unchurched tend to be less engaged with the world than are churched adults.

Technology has become a significant part of most people's lives. Our evaluation of the technology owned by the unchurched shows that they have a ownership pattern virtually identical to that of the churched. The only difference worth mentioning was a slightly lower rate of ownership of cell phones, but the gap was not big enough to indicate a significant behavioral difference.

Interestingly, about one-third of the unchurched say that using the Internet has helped them to make and maintain friendships. Two-thirds of the unchurched who said this were under the age of 35. Also of importance was the finding that one-fifth of the unchurched adults noted that the Internet is a source of information they use regarding spirituality and matters of faith. Again, this tended to be a behavior of younger adults.

The Unchurched and Charity

Even an examination of the types of nonprofit organizations (NPOs) the unchurched have supported financially in their recent pasts shows that there are relatively few lifestyle differences in comparison to churched adults. The unchurched demonstrated a slightly lower inclination to give to each category of NPOs, with one exception: environmental groups. In that case, the unchurched were twice as likely to have given to organizations focused on defending the environment. Otherwise, they were slightly less likely to have donated to educational and youth agencies, to social welfare organizations, to medical and health care NPOs, to religious entities (other than churches) and to public service groups.

We also explored the perceptions of the types of organizations the unchurched feel are most worth supporting. Their attitudes in this regard tell us something about the qualities they deem to be most appealing—and, potentially, what they may be looking for in a church.

Surprisingly, their attitudes were hard to distinguish from those of the churched. Nine out of 10 said they seek an organization that is known for integrity. Eight out of 10 (78 percent) look for a compelling mission and vision that defines the activity of the organization (slightly less than the 86 percent of the churched said this was very important, but generally similar in significance). Eight out of 10 also said they evaluate the fiscal responsibility of an organization, and seven out of 10 look for strong, creative problem-solving skills. Only one-third said that having an ethnically diverse staff or leadership group makes a big difference. The least stock was placed in whether the leader of the organization is "articulate and charismatic": Only 12 percent said they deem that to be very important. That, too, is slightly lower than the importance assigned it by the churched, but out of the six items listed, it remains the lowest rated item for both groups.

How They See Their Priorities

Some of the entryways into the lives of unchurched people become clearer once we examine their priorities in life and how satisfied they are with their current state of life in each of those areas. Table 5.5 presents information regarding the life outcomes that the unchurched deem to be most desirable.

It is obvious that among the potential outcomes we tested, the response levels of the unchurched were significantly different from those of the churched on 17 of the 21 items! Most intriguing of all is the nature of the distinctions. The unchurched showed less enthusiasm than did the churched respondents in relation to 13 of those 17 items. Is it because they have set their sights lower? Is it because they are more realistic about what to expect? We cannot tell, but we do know that the life outcomes more compelling to the unchurched than to the churched related to leading "the good life." The unchurched were more desirous of having a comfortable lifestyle, a high-paying job, traveling for pleasure and owning a large home. For achievement-oriented people with a spiritual vacuum in their lives, these goals make sense.

Table 5.5
What Is Most Desirable for Their Future
(% who said this is "very desirable" for their life in the future)

	unchurched	churched	teens
having good physical health	85%	93%	87%
living with a high degree of integrity	73	85	71
having one marriage partner for life	70	85	82
having close, personal friendships	69	78	84
having a clear purpose for living	64	80	77
having a close relationship with God	44	84	66
having a satisfying sex life with your marriage partner	62	64	55
having a comfortable lifestyle	66	59	83
living close to your family and relatives	52	64	49
having children	48	58	54
being deeply committed to the Christian faith	20	70	50
being knowledgeable about current events	40	54	NA
making a difference in the world	37	52	56
being personally active in a church	11	57	43
having a college degree	38	42	88
influencing other people's lives	31	40	56
working in a high-paying job	36	26	55
traveling throughout the world for pleasure	31	24	NA
owning a large home	25	18	28
owning the latest household technology and electronic equipment	8	9	27
achieving fame or public recognition	8	5	18
sample size	327	675	605

Another significant revelation is that a majority of the churched listed the key faith outcomes tested as personal priorities, while only a
minority of the unchurched did so. The churched are twice as likely to
say they want a close relationship with God and more than three times
as likely to say they want to be deeply committed to the Christian faith.
The churched are five times more likely to say they want to be active in
a church, and they are about one-third more likely to express an interest
in making a difference in the world. Clearly, as most of the unchurched
chart their future, faith is not a major concern. We do not want to overlook the small core who do view faith development and connection as a
priority—a group that constitutes perhaps a fifth of the segment—but in
terms of the hierarchy of felt needs among most of the unchurched,
faith development is missing-in-action.

They Look at the Future

The other major takeaway from the data relates to the nature of what the
unchurched are most focused upon for the future. There are seven items
that a majority listed as priorities. Those items deal with health, relationships, purpose and character. The items that did not make the
upper echelon of importance, besides faith, relate to family, service and
leisure.

In passing, also notice what teenagers listed as future priorities. In
relation to spiritual matters, they tend to lie somewhere between the
unchurched and the churched. They are typically interested in having a
close relationship with God (two-thirds desire that outcome), half are
interested in being deeply committed to the Christian faith and somewhat less than half would like to be active in a church. They tend to be
very relational individuals—in fact, relationships are the driving force
behind many of their choices and dreams in life—and therefore they
hope to have influence in people's lives and to make a difference in the
world. But most teens are not sure that being connected with a church
will enhance that opportunity. Do not lose sight of the fact that most
teenagers are currently churched—they have a higher church participation rate than adults do! Yet they are not inclined to position organized
religion at the hub of their futures.[1]

They Weigh Their Success

The life priorities described above gain greater context when we examine the satisfaction levels detailed in table 5.6. At Barna Research, we asked a national sample of the unchurched to describe how satisfied they were with each of 15 dimensions of life. Using a six-point scale to convey their responses (ranging from "extremely satisfied" to "not at all satisfied"), the results are again enlightening. First, notice that a majority of the unchurched were either "extremely" or "very satisfied" in relation to only two of the 15 dimensions (i.e., their marriage and their personal character). However, there was not a single item among the list tested for which even 7 out of every 10 people were highly satisfied.

The value of the satisfaction ratings, however, is magnified when we compare them with the levels of importance assigned to each of the dimensions. For instance, we can see that only one out of every five unchurched adults is highly satisfied with his or her community involvement, but we also find that such efforts are a low priority to the unchurched. So it is not likely that most unchurched people will do much about the low satisfaction they have in this regard. The same conclusion can be reached regarding satisfaction with their level of influence, spiritual life, current job and educational achievement: Their limited degree of satisfaction is mitigated by the comparatively low priority each of those items represents in their lives.

They Rank Top Priorities for the Future

The five dimensions that a majority of the unchurched defined as top priorities for their future were tested. We can see that while three-quarters said their personal character is important, only half of them felt that their character is measuring up to their own standards. Seven out of 10 unchurched individuals said having a successful marriage is critical, but just two-thirds were highly satisfied with the condition of their own marriage. Seven out of 10 labeled friendships as a top priority, but only half were highly satisfied with their current relationships. Two-thirds said that the overall quality of their life was a key consideration, yet barely 2 out of 5 said they were highly satisfied with that dimension of their lives. Almost two-thirds claimed that having a satisfying sex life with their marriage partner was of top significance, but just half as many felt they were achieving that outcome. The biggest gap relates to personal health. More than four out of five unchurched adults said good health was a very desirable life product, but only one-third of them were extremely or very satisfied with the present state of their health.

In other words, we can identify areas of life that unchurched adults deem to be highly significant for their future, and we find that they are at least moderately disenchanted with how they are doing in each area. Whether or not they would be willing to take direction from a church to enhance their lives in regard to that area is another issue altogether.

Table 5.6
Satisfaction Levels with Dimensions of Life

	unchurched	churched
your marriage*	65%	59%
personal character	52	51
family life	50	52
career choice*	48	49
friendships	47	51
overall lifestyle	42	41
current job*	40	44
educational achievement	39	38
spiritual life	35	45
sex life	34	36
health	32	38
leisure time	31	23
financial condition	29	25
level of influence	25	27
community involvement	19	22
sample size	287	746

(*indicates this was asked only among people to whom it was relevant)

We also asked the unchurched to describe future possibilities that they consider to be most exciting. The items that topped the list included providing a good life for their children, experiencing technological breakthroughs, improved government performance and better physical health. Items related to career or financial success, when grouped together (described by about one-quarter of the group), emerged as the most alluring possibility. Only one out of every 50 unchurched people mentioned positive spiritual experiences or progress as one of the possibilities that he or she found to be most exciting.

When we followed that up with a question about the future possibilities that troubled or worried them most, the dominant concern was personal physical threats (war, street violence and physical crime). This issue outscored the second-most common concern (environmental decay) by a three-to-one margin. Again, this is an issue that relates closely to their concerns about quality of life and the ability to define themselves through their accomplishments.

How to Mine the Data

So what does all of this information tell us about the unchurched?

Generally, these are individuals who do not see themselves as weak, needy or broken people. They are achievement-oriented, driven people who work with other human beings but are not as deeply concerned about people as the typical church person seems to be. As a group, they are quite matter-of-fact about life and would probably have a hard time understanding notions like "being controlled by the Spirit" or "trusting God to direct your paths." They are self-reliant and have become comfortable with that approach to life.

Driven though they are, life is not producing the quality of experience that they desire. Most unchurched people could identify a half dozen or so areas in their lives in which their experiences are falling far short of their expectations. This undoubtedly contributes to their stress and frustration with life. Since many of these individuals are independent, self-reliant, problem-solving types of people, they are constantly scanning the terrain for alternatives that might raise their fulfillment level a notch or two.

Although they have a spiritual side, they are not highly religious and few of them are seeking to increase their spiritual focus. If they do, their inclination would be to find groups that have a rather lenient, laissez-faire theological approach, since their desire would be to retain control and authority over their lives. They are also likely to search for churches that address the issues of greatest interest or concern to them—matters related to quality of life, means to achievement and development of better relationships without having to become highly relational people.

As we reach out to unchurched people, we should expect them to be generally ambivalent toward organized religion and even resistant to the ways of the Church. We should not take their reactions personally. They are consistent with who they are and how they have coped with life to this point. Only a small percentage of the unchurched actively seek a deeper relationship with God, one that will allow Him to exert greater control over their lives. They are not terribly interested in joining groups, and their driven, independent nature makes them suspicious of people who suddenly strive to build friendships with them. They are not unreachable, but spiritual development is not on their to-do list. Influencing them with the things of God will take time, prayer and an intelligent strategy.

Note

1. For more information about spiritual activities, inclinations and expectations of teenagers see our research described in my book *Real Teens* (Ventura, CA: Regal Books, 2001).

THREE-QUARTERS OF THE UNCHURCHED BELIEVE THAT

A. the miracles of the Bible actually took place.

B. Jesus was born of a virgin.

C. God helps those who help themselves.

D. the Bible is the literal Word of God.

E. all of the religious groups of the world teach the same principles.

F. Satan is not a living being, but only a symbol of evil.

CHAPTER 6

THE FAITH OF THE UNCHURCHED

Every time they step on the brakes of their cars, they exhibit tremendous faith in gadgets that most of them know nothing about. Each time they go out in public, they demonstrate faith in the behavior and morals of humankind, believing that they will not be shot or mugged. When they take a bite of food that has been prepared at a restaurant by a chef they never see or do not know, they show the faith they possess, believing that it was properly cooked and not poisoned. Each time they make a bank deposit, they engage in an act of faith, believing that their money will be returned to them, perhaps with interest. The issue is not whether they have faith; rather, it is where they place their faith.

There is no easy answer to this question of what the unchurched place their ultimate faith in. Most unchurched people have some relationship with religion, spirituality and faith matters. However, for them the role and nature of faith looks and operates differently than it does for the two-thirds of the people who are churched.

IN THE BEGINNING

The cornerstone of Christian wisdom is the Bible. Christian beliefs and life practices are to be in concert with those described in God's Word. More than 9 out of 10 churched people own more than one Bible, and many of them actually read it at least once a week.

Most of America's unchurched adults, in spite of their limited interest in organized religion, also own a Bible (75 percent). Two out of five (39 percent) of them believe that the Bible is either the literal Word of

God that contains no errors and means exactly what it says or that it is the inspired, inerrant Word that is completely accurate but cannot be taken literally because it uses symbolic language in some instances. That is a much smaller slice of Bible believers than can be found within the churched community (67 percent), but nevertheless it represents a sizable foundation on which to build. In addition, one out of five unchurched adults contends that the Bible was inspired by God but contains some historical and factual errors. The other one-third of the unchurched assert that the Bible is not God's Word; rather, they contend that it is a book that was conceived and written by humans and is filled with errors and fallacies.

Whether or not they perceive it to be God's Word, very few of the unchurched read the Bible on a regular basis. Only 3 percent claim to read it daily. By contrast, 17 percent of the churched say that they read the Bible every day.

Overall, 15 percent of the unchurched read the Bible at least once a week, 10 percent once a month, 12 percent once a quarter, 18 percent once or twice a year and 21 percent on rare occasions. The remaining one-quarter never read the Bible.

One reason why so many unchurched adults may ignore the Bible is because of the version that they own. Without intending to denigrate the value of any particular translation, we know from extensive research on Bible usage that certain versions are easier than others for people to understand. The most difficult to comprehend is the *King James Version*. In spite of that fact, the *King James Version* remains the most widely used version in the country, although this is slowly changing as the avalanche of modern translations becomes better known and more widely trusted.

> One reason why so many unchurched adults may ignore the Bible is because of the version that they own.

Our surveys among the unchurched shows that while three-quarters of them own a *King James Version* Bible, a little less than half of them own another, more readable version. The low readership levels may be related to the fact that 6 out of 10 unchurched people consider the *King James Version* to be their primary reading version. Not even one-tenth of unchurched adults named another version. In contrast, three-quarters of churched people own a *King James Version*, but an even larger proportion owns at least one of the many modern translations. The *King James Version* is still the most commonly owned version, outpacing its nearest competitor by more than a two-to-one margin. But only one-third of the churched call it their primary translation.

Table 6.1
Bible Reading Frequency

	unchurched	churched
weekly	15%	50%
monthly	10	14
quarterly	12	11
once/twice a year	18	7
less than once a year	21	4
never	25	8
sample size	273	727

WHAT DO THEY BELIEVE?

Indisputably, the unchurched are a study in contradictions when it comes to matters of faith. Most unchurched people are not overly religious or spiritual, yet 70 percent call themselves Christian. Three-quarters of them own a Bible, but few read the contents. Almost half of them state that having a close, personal relationship with God is one of their top priorities in life, but surprisingly few of them do much to facilitate that bond.

To get beyond the apparent inconsistencies and complexities and figure out how to minister to unchurched people, we must understand their perception of the Christian faith. Many of them think of the Bible as an outdated book of rules, but a number of them believe it to be a relevant, useful guidebook to modern living. How they apply the perceived insights from Scripture depends on what they believe those insights to be. Let's examine the religious beliefs of the unchurched.

General Beliefs

Two-thirds of the unchurched consider their religious faith to be very important. Almost two-thirds of those individuals give strong (as opposed to moderate) affirmation to this notion. The older a person is, the more likely he or she is to possess this view. In fact, only one out of every four Baby Busters (adults age 35 and under) concurred strongly with this view, compared to a majority of the 50-plus unchurched. The significance of faith was more strongly affirmed by political conservatives than by those who hold moderate or liberal views.

Consistent with their own low-key pursuits of faith, most unchurched adults say that a person can lead a full and satisfying life even if he or she does not incorporate or develop a faith. Six out of ten unchurched adults accept this idea as accurate, while one-third rejects it. For most people, then, faith is an optional pursuit, a kind of bonus benefit that may prove to be useful.

Beliefs About Deity

The more we explore the beliefs of the unchurched, the more contradictions we encounter. Seven out of 10 unchurched adults believe that God originally created the universe. The nature of the God in which they believe, however, leaves much to be desired. Less than half of the unchurched (47 percent) believe that "God is the all-powerful, all-knowing, perfect creator of the universe who still rules the world today."

One must wonder how the 23 percent who claim that God created the world but does not rule it today would explain this view. Did God create the world, watch for a while and then vanish? Did He create the universe but then lose His dominion over it? Have these individuals really thought through the spiritual implications of this perspective?

Two out of 10 unchurched adults say that "God" refers to a higher state of consciousness that people may achieve. One out of 10 contends that God is the full realization of human potential. Six percent say everyone is God. Another 6 percent believe that there are many different gods, and 8 percent simply state that there is no such thing as God.

> Two out of 10 unchurched adults say that "God" refers to a higher state of consciousness.

Beliefs about Jesus are no more consistent. Two-thirds of the unchurched contend that Jesus was born to a virgin. But His miraculous birthing fails to impress many of them, half of whom believe that Jesus sinned while He was on Earth. Half also argue that He was crucified and died but that He never had a physical resurrection. The sinful nature of Jesus is attested to most heartily by people under 45 and by individuals who earn more than $75,000 annually.

They do not do much better with the Holy Spirit. Almost two-thirds of the unchurched deny the existence of the Third Person, saying that the Holy Spirit is a symbol of God's presence or power but is not a living entity. Interestingly, the answers of the churched were not much different from those of the unchurched.

Beliefs About Other Spiritual Forces

The unchurched are not only bewildered over the Trinity; they also demonstrate tremendous confusion regarding one other spiritual power: Satan. Seven out of 10 contend that Satan does not exist but is simply a symbol used to connote evil. Even a majority of the churched populace believe this lie!

To their credit, most unchurched individuals (69 percent) do believe that angels exist and can affect people's lives. Perhaps we should credit CBS television for this widespread theological insight—they are the ones who bring us *Touched by an Angel*.

Isn't it interesting, and disheartening, that more people—churched and unchurched, believer and nonbeliever—accept the existence of angels than believe in the reality of the Holy Spirit or Satan?

Beliefs About the Bible

In a rare display of theological consistency, we found that 38 percent of the unchurched agreed that the Bible is totally accurate in all that it teaches, which is nearly identical to the 39 percent who said that they perceive the Bible to be either the literal Word of God or His inspired Word without error. However, those individuals were divided among those who strongly agree that the Bible is completely accurate (22 percent) and those who are only somewhat convinced of that truth (16 percent). Of course, a majority (52 percent) do not buy into the idea at all, and another 10 percent do not know what to think.

There is a moderately strong relationship between socioeconomic status and agreement with the Bible's accuracy: The less education a person has completed and the less income a person earns, the more likely he or she is to accept the Bible as accurate. Stated differently, the more wealthy a person is, the more skeptical he or she is about the Bible. There is also a substantial regional distinction in this regard. Unchurched Southerners are considerably more likely than unchurched adults from other regions to accept the accuracy of Scripture. Almost half of the unchurched people in the South (48 percent) accept the Bible as accurate, compared to only one-third of all other unchurched (35 percent).

About half of the unchurched (55 percent) agree that all of the miracles described in the Bible actually took place. Apparently, the difficulty that roughly one-sixth of the skeptics have with believing biblical content is not related to doubts about the miracles.

Beliefs About Salvation

The spiritual deception of the unchurched is perhaps most extensive regarding salvation. In broad terms, we find that they generally reject the necessity of accepting Christ as savior and instead believe that through good deeds a person can earn his or her way into Heaven—or even that after death there will not be any condemnation of anyone, no matter how a person lived life.

The contradiction here is that only one out of every four unchurched adults argues that sin is an outdated concept. Most of these people accept the existence of sin but do not believe that sin will have an eternal effect on an individual's destiny. Fewer than one out of five unchurched believe that there is no afterlife, and the remainder are divided between believing that everyone will experience the same, generally positive outcome and believing that a person can earn eternal salvation through a preponderance of good deeds.

Amazingly, most of the unchurched believe that they will go to heaven after they die, although few attribute that gift to the grace of God, their own profession of faith and their own acknowledgment of sin.

Beliefs About Other Faiths

Slightly more than half of the unchurched believe that all of the major faith groups in the world teach the same basic principles. An identical percentage of them (54 percent) believes that it does not matter what faith group you associate with because of the similarity in the principles being taught. This one-world-religion perspective is particularly prevalent among unchurched people under 40 years of age.

Beliefs About Personal Responsibility

When it comes to what people perceive about their personal responsibilities as they relate to faith, there is some good news and some bad news. The bad news is that three-fourths of the unchurched believe that the Bible actually teaches that God helps those who help themselves. That line was first said by a seventeenth-century English poet and later popularized by Benjamin Franklin, whom few people have argued was one of God's inspired scribes.[1] This perspective is a natural fit among people who are admittedly self-sufficient and independent. It is also a perfect summary of contemporary American theology: The world revolves around us, and God is welcome to piggyback on our efforts if He so desires. Since this is the "bad news" paragraph, let me add one more disturbing tidbit: The response of churched people is identical on this issue to that of the unchurched.

The good news is that relatively few of the unchurched (25 percent) believe that they have a responsibility to tell other people their religious beliefs. I am not rejecting evangelism, but I am thrilled that most of those who do not hold biblically accurate views have chosen to keep those views to themselves. The question that their opinion raises, of course, is whether they are silent about their beliefs simply because they are so uncertain about them and those beliefs are not important to them or because they believe that all people should keep their beliefs to themselves.

Beliefs As They Relate to Moral Truth

Whether absolute moral truth exists is a fundamental issue that determines the health or illness of a culture. Other research we conducted throughout the 1990s identified our nation's movement toward the rejection of moral absolutes and the acceptance of moral relativism. Sadly, we have seen that born-again Christians are nearly as likely as nonbelievers to reject moral absolutes, in spite of their professed allegiance to the Bible.

Given that, it should not be shocking to learn that the unchurched have gravitated toward relativism as their philosophy of choice. Only 1 out of every 4 unchurched adults believes there is absolute moral truth that is knowable and unchanging. One-third believe that all truth is relative to the person and circumstances. Another 3 out of 10 say that they have never thought about it—and, consequently, they side with the default position of our culture, relativism. The remaining one-eighth simply have not arrived at a conclusion on the matter, although they also typically live in cooperation with the default position.

The unchurched do not regularly reflect upon moral truth. Only one-third say that they have spent any time at all thinking about the matter. In total, just 1 out of every 4 unchurched individuals characterizes figuring out the existence of moral absolutes as very important. A larger share (one-third) says the matter is not important to them. A plurality (4 out of 10) describes this issue as somewhat important.

These figures, in conjunction with other studies we have conducted, indicate that only a handful of unchurched adults operate with a biblical worldview as a decision-making filter in their life.

Table 6.2
What Unchurched Americans Believe
(N=1175)

statement	AST	ASW	DSW	DST
my religious faith is very important in my life	42%	24%	17%	14%
the Bible is totally accurate in all of its teachings	22	16	24	28
you, personally, have a responsibility to tell other people your religious beliefs	13	12	22	50
the devil, or Satan, is not a living being but is a symbol of evil	41	29	9	18
if a person is generally good, or does enough good things for others during their life, he will earn a place in Heaven	37	32	12	18
when He lived on Earth, Jesus Christ was human and committed sins, like other people	22	26	10	28
it doesn't matter what religious faith you follow because they all teach the same lessons	27	27	16	26
the Holy Spirit is a symbol of God's presence or power but is not a living entity	35	28	9	16
after he was crucified and died, Jesus Christ did not return to life physically	29	18	12	25
the Bible teaches that God helps those who help themselves	50	26	5	10
all people will experience the same outcome after death, regardless of their religious beliefs	37	15	20	19

Continued on next page

statement	AST	ASW	DSW	DST
there are some crimes, sins or other things which people might do which cannot be forgiven by God	24	16	16	35
angels exist and influence people's lives	35	34	9	12
the universe was originally created by God	53	18	9	12
the whole idea of sin is outdated	12	11	19	52
you can lead a full and satisfying life even if you do not include spiritual development in your life	35	24	14	21
people who do not consciously accept Jesus Christ as their savior will be condemned to hell after they die	15	8	18	54
Jesus Christ was born to a virgin	47	18	9	14
all of the miracles described in the Bible actually happened	38	17	16	20
all of the major religious groups of the world teach the same principles	27	27	16	26

KEY: AST = agree strongly; ASW = agree somewhat;
DSW = disagree somewhat; DST = disagree strongly.

NOTE: Percentages may not add up to 100 percent because the "don't know" response is not included in this table.

LEVEL OF COMMITMENT

Not surprisingly, among the 70 percent who label themselves Christian, the commitment level is not very high. Overall, just 11 percent say that they are absolutely committed to Christianity, and another 29 percent say they are moderately committed. Most of the unchurched are even less committed: 15 percent say "not too committed" and 44 percent say "not at all committed."

If we project the statistics to the entire segment of the unchurched and add a couple of other facts from our research, we arrive at the following profile:

- 14 percent are atheists
- 16 percent align themselves with other faith groups
- 8 percent call themselves Christian and say they are "absolutely committed"
- 20 percent call themselves Christian and say they are "moderately committed"
- 11 percent call themselves Christian and say they are "not too committed"
- 31 percent call themselves Christian and say they are "not at all committed"

Certainly one of the warnings to us inherent in these numbers is that when a person describes himself or herself as a Christian, we cannot take the statement at face value. Because the term "Christian" has become so generic in our culture, we need to probe a bit to discover what type of Christian the individual is which may range from the nominal Christian to a deeply devout follower of Jesus. There are many shades of alleged Christianity in between those end points.

Notice that only one out of every seven unchurched adults is an atheist.

> **O**nly one out of every seven unchurched adults is an atheist.

Naturally, those individuals will require an entirely different strategy if we are to get them to connect with the Church. Knowing that six out of seven people at least have some self-perception of a religious connection paves the way for constructive and fruitful outreach built on a foundation of basic belief in God.

Keep in mind that 15 percent of the unchurched adults in our country say they will "definitely" return to church within the next three months, and another one-quarter (23 percent) say they "probably" will return. This is a return to levels we measured in 1986 and substantially higher than the levels measured in 1990 and 1995. Millions of unchurched adults are open to the possibility of reattaching to a community of faith.

Our experience in researching people's projected behavior tells us that the "likely to return" estimates are overly optimistic. A more realistic assessment of the number of adults who might return to a church is in the 13 to 16 percent range. The experience those individuals have at the church they visit may well determine whether they stay connected or leave again—perhaps for good.

Born Again, Bored Again

We also discovered that almost one out of five unchurched adults—18 percent—is a born-again Christian. By this we mean that they say they have made a personal commitment to Jesus Christ that is still important in their lives today, and that they know they will go to heaven when they die because they have confessed their sins and accepted Jesus Christ as their savior. (We do not ask people to designate themselves as "born-again." We categorize them as such according to how they answer the two items just described regarding salvation.)[2]

A Very High Dropout Rate

There are some significant implications to the fact that one-fifth of the unchurched are born again. One of the considerations relates to church dropouts and retention. The fact that such a substantial slice of the adult born-again population—about 15 percent of the total—could walk away from the church without any intention of returning ought to make us pause and reflect on how we can more effectively retain believers within the church. It is one thing for a person to accept a credit card and then return it, join a health club and then drop the membership, or register to vote and then fail to show up on election days. But in this survey we were talking about an eternal relationship with God Himself and maintaining that relationship in the company of other believers. What can we learn from the dropouts to prevent future defections from the Church—not simply to salvage the institution, but for the sake of the spiritual health of every member and for the good of the Kingdom?

A second consideration concerns the prospects for church growth. If just the born again adults who are unchurched returned to the church, that would represent an influx of more than 12 million adults (along with perhaps another 4 to 6 million children). If we were to distribute those 12 million adults evenly among the 324,000 Protestant churches in America, the increase would amount to 37 adults per church. Given that the average church has only 90 adult members, this growth would constitute more than a 40 percent expansion of the average church. (Of course, these assumptions are for illustrative purposes; if the scenario described were to occur, it would stand as one of God's most amazing miracles. Guiding those 12 million people back to the Church would go down in the history books as one of the great revivals of all time.)

Reenlist the Runaways
Even if all 12 million unchurched believers do not return to the Church within the next few years, a significant proportion of them could be attracted back. We found that the dominant reasons for their avoidance of the Church are lack of time and lack of interest: these two motivating factors cover about three out of five of the unchurched believers. Very few of these people stay away because of bad past experiences (less than 5 percent); more often, they duck the church because of irrelevant past experiences. Providing them with a high-value experience—genuine worship, relevant discipleship, sincere and caring relationships, meaningful opportunities for gift-based service, loving accountability and an environment ripe for productive evangelism—would ring the bells of millions of these wayward family members. Convincing them that they could have such a worthwhile experience would perhaps be the toughest challenge in the process; but if we deliver the goods, they are likely to reenlist.

Spiritual Involvement and Exposure

Having just railed against the superficial faith commitment of the unchurched, let me now show that few of them have completely insulated themselves from religious exposure.

The defining characteristic of the unchurched, of course, is that they do not attend church services. However, they voluntarily gain exposure to a host of other religious and spiritual influences. Here is a list of some of those experiences.

- Half of the unchurched pray to God in a typical week.
- Three out of 10 have a quiet time or devotional time during an average week.
- One out of every seven reads from the Bible during the week; one out of four does so in a typical month. Roughly the same number reads from a book of sacred literature other than the Bible in an average month.
- One out of every 10 is engaged in a spiritual mentoring process.
- Very few engage in group activities such as Sunday school classes (2 percent attend in a typical week) or a small group (3 percent).
- One out of every 10 purchased Christian music in the preceding year.
- Three out of 10 watch religious television programming in a typical month.
- One out of four listen to Christian radio programming during an average month.
- One out of five read a Christian magazine during an average 30-day period.

When we put it all together, we discover that slightly more than three-quarters of the unchurched have some type of self-initiated interaction with religious activity or information. There is a reasonable chance of reaching these individuals with a positive, life-changing message—if we are strategic about the process.

THE LIKELIHOOD OF RETURNING TO A CHRISTIAN CHURCH IN THE NEAR FUTURE

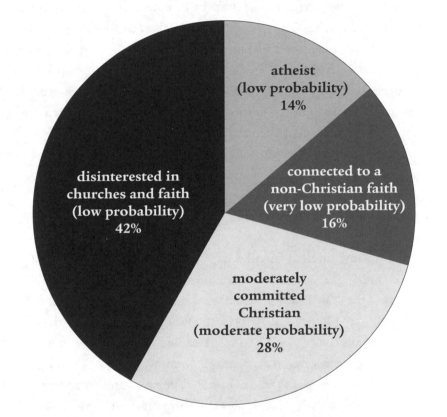

WHAT DOES THIS ALL MEAN?

There are significant opportunities to penetrate the unchurched market with God's love and truth. While there is a hardcore segment that is not ready to be reached yet, there are millions of people disconnected from the Church who are ripe for reconnection. One out of every seven is likely to visit a church in the coming three to six months, seeking a spiritual home. Twice as many (one-third of the unchurched) admit that they are more likely to look for spiritual answers to address the problems and challenges they face in life than they were three years ago. The unchurched are not going to come to us, but if we initiate appropriate contact, deliver on our promises and fulfill their spiritual needs, millions of unchurched people can be aligned with a Christian church.

To make the most of the existing opportunities, and to create additional ones, we need to recognize that the unchurched market is divided into self-defined niches. The people within each of those niches have different degrees of likelihood of joining the Church. Overall, 16 percent are associated with other, non-Christian religions (this group has the lowest probability of aligning with a local church); 14 percent are atheists (also a low probability of joining us); 28 percent think of themselves as committed Christians (highest probability of reconnecting); and 42 percent are neither interested in organized religion nor consider faith to be a major issue in life (low probability of returning to a church).

What can you do to increase the interest of the unchurched in returning to the fold? Here are some possibilities.

- Give an unchurched friend a copy of a modern translation of the Bible. The *New King James Version*, the *New International Version*, the *New Living Translation* or another recent entry into the Bible market might help God's Word come alive for these individuals. Such a gift must be handled deftly or else it may seem too pushy or even arrogant. If you have the chance to discuss life's issues with the unchurched person—and you identify key issues on which you have differing opinions—you might "tease" him or her into examining his or her Bible. You could explain how you arrived at your stand through the application of biblical content, and you might offer to give him or her a user-friendly version.
- Take Peter's exhortation seriously: Always be prepared to give a reason for the hope that is within you (1 Pet. 3:15). Most Americans, even the unchurched, are seeking hope. Think through how you could sensitively but persuasively (not offensively or aggressively) communicate the reasons for your faith. Be sure to use practical, nonreligious terminology.
- Grace is a concept that millions of Americans do not under-

stand. Yet it is a cornerstone concept for people to comprehend if they are going to accept God's grace offered to everyone through the death and resurrection of Jesus. Reflect on practical ways to describe what both the concept and the experience of that grace has meant to you.

- Learn to listen for the underlying foundations of people's arguments. Often you will discover that their fundamental assumptions include the rejection of absolute moral truth. Without becoming argumentative or philosophically obtuse, develop the skill of identifying the fallacy of people's truth assumptions, and learn how to propose inoffensively an alternative for them to consider. Paul was a great role model in this regard: He sought to understand the cultural assumptions of his audience, and then he discussed a divergent but reasonable point of view in ways that made him interesting (see Acts 17).

- Before you invite your unchurched associates to a worship service, take the time to examine your church through their eyes. Is your church accessible and comprehensible to someone who is not a believer, has little knowledge of the Bible or is unfamiliar with how the church works? Our studies have found that sometimes we have done more harm by inviting unchurched people to a particular church—i.e., one that was unsuited to their needs or unprepared to reach out to them—than would have been done by enveloping them in a web of faith-based relationships or exposing them to carefully chosen spiritual experiences other than worship services or regular church programs. There is a church that is right for everyone, but it may not be yours. After assessing your church through their eyes, if you discover that it is not really unchurched-friendly, take the initiative to do something about it. Your church can change for the better without compromising its vision, values or beliefs.

Notes

1. Benjamin Franklin [Richard Saunders, pseudo.], *Poor Richard's Almanac* (Philadelphia, PA: self-published, 1757), prefix.

2. In all of our research and throughout this book, the term "born again" is based on asking people's response to two survey questions. In the first question we ask people, "Have you ever made a personal commitment to Jesus Christ that is still important in your life today?" If they answer yes, we then pose the second question, which relates to what they believe will happen to them after they die. One of the seven options we offer is "After I die, I know I will go to heaven because I have confessed my sins and have accepted Jesus Christ as my Savior." We then classify people who provide that answer as born-again Christians. We do not ask people if they consider themselves to be born again. We also do not truly know who is born again—only God does—but we use this process of estimation to give us a sense of what is happening spiritually among those who rely on God's grace rather than works or universalism for their salvation.

WHAT DO MOST UNCHURCHED PEOPLE PREFER TO BE CALLED?

A. inquirer
B. seeker
C. lost
D. non-Christian
E. unbeliever
F. explorer

CHAPTER 7

WHAT THE UNCHURCHED WANT FROM A CHURCH

Family counselors tell us that one of the greatest destroyers of marriages is the failure of spouses to communicate with each other. Conflict and disappointment are inevitable results in any relationship, but the key is not to eliminate their occurrence as much as to address them effectively as challenges to be overcome. Understanding the nature and emergence of a problem or threat is crucial in developing appropriate and timely solutions.

The same principle holds true in regards to reaching and ministering to the unchurched. We cannot hope to be effective in our efforts to guide them to the Cross and integrate them into a community of faith if we do not comprehend the issues that keep them away from the Church and the personal needs and expectations they possess regarding spirituality and church life. In this chapter, I will examine our research on what unchurched people want from a church.

THE ENTRY POINT

One of the disturbing revelations that emerges from our research is that most pastors, and a large share of Christian individuals, restrict their thinking about how to reach the unchurched. They tend to limit outreach to attracting them to a worship service. Given that the fundamentals of authentic Christian living encompass worship, discipleship, stewardship, evangelism, service and relationships with other believers, the significance of the worship service is not to be dismissed. However, pushing to get unchurched people reconnected with God and His Church solely by means of a worship service is shortsighted.

When we examine the attitudes of the unchurched, we discover that a majority of them indicate that the best way to get them connected to a Christian church is *not* through a worship service. While it was the number one answer, only 4 out of 10 unchurched adults said that attending a worship service would be their preferred means of access. One out of 5 said they would prefer to connect through special events that were open to all people, both regulars and outsiders. One out of 7 expressed an interest in participating in community service activities. Fewer than 1 out of 10 listed various other options, including small classes held specifically for visitors, small groups and Sunday school classes.

Younger adults expressed the least interest in worship services. Their answers revealed an interest in more relational experiences, such as community outreach projects or special events that connect people from outside and inside the church. Worship services had their greatest appeal among blacks, residents of the Midwest and individuals who fall into the category of the "cautious" behavioral type (see chapter 5).

Table 7.1
The Desired Entry Point to Attract the Unchurched

worship service	40%
special event open to all people	19
community outreach activity	15
small class for church visitors	6
small group at someone's home	5
adult Sunday School class	4
not sure; depends on situation	11

The point to take away from these statistics is not that it is bad to invite unchurched people to worship services or that they will not attend them. The data suggests that a substantial proportion of the unchurched expect to reconnect with a church through that very means. The key revelation is that there must be multiple routes of entry available to unchurched people. Just as some people get back into physical exercise through different means—joining an aerobics class, jogging, swimming, using machines that promote heart exertion, playing racquetball, participating in team sports and so forth—so Americans will choose to return to church through various approaches. We cannot afford to put all of our eggs in the "worship basket" if we are serious about reaching as many people as we can for the kingdom of God.

THE PEOPLE FACTOR

One perspective became very clear through our two-year study of the unchurched: Their likelihood of returning to and remaining at a church largely depends upon the nature of the people in any particular congregation. Theology matters, but in the minds of the unchurched (and, quite frankly, most of the churched), the friendly and caring nature of the people matters more.

One veteran of the Church who had dropped out and was considering a return described it this way:

> I probably wouldn't know good religious teaching from bad, or a great sermon from one that breaks every rule in the preaching manual. But I sure know nice people from jerks, and real people from hypocrites. I would stay at a church with lousy teaching but genuinely friendly people—people who got to know me and cared about me and respected my needs and boundaries—before I would stay at a place with perfect teaching and lousy people.

Good Memories
About two-thirds of the unchurched told us that when they recall the things they liked about the churches they had visited in the past, they remember the people most vividly. They felt drawn to the community

and to the authentic faith struggles of the individuals in those places. They may not have understood or embraced the same values as all of the church regulars, but they respected the honest efforts members made to clarify and incorporate those values.

Slightly more than one-third of the unchurched recalled with warmth the preaching and teaching at the churches they had attended; but for most people, the intellectual or substantive emphasis was less meaningful than the emotional or relational emphasis of churches. The environment of the church—how formal or casual, how inviting or uninviting, how physically comfortable or uncomfortable, how uplifting or negative the atmosphere—was fondly remembered by one out of every five of the unchurched. Almost as many cited different elements of the church's corporate ministry, such as the music or traditions. Only a few (5 percent) ranked programs or ministry activities of the church as a draw.

The Personal Touch

The significance of the personal touch at church is especially intriguing in light of our finding that unchurched people are not as relational as typical churched individuals. The focus on relational connections also raises the question of why unchurched people left the church they were attending if they felt so cared for and connected. The answer turns out to be that the unchurched were not sufficiently tied into the lives of the people at the church—they did not feel completely connected. Combined with the other pressures they were facing in their lives, the limited importance they attached to preaching and Bible teaching, and their ambivalence toward worship, they did not feel compelled to continue to be part of a church.

THE LOST AND NOT FOUND

One of the more enlightening insights from our research concerns the language that we use to describe unchurched people, especially those who do not know Christ as their savior. Our observation of churches across the country is that one of the most common terms used is "the

lost." We have many popular expressions: "Lost people matter to God."
"Our goal is to reach the lost at any cost." "We must bring the lost into
a right relationship with God." "Bring your lost friends to church."
"Until you build bridges to the lost people in our community, there is no
clear pathway for them to follow on the route to spiritual wholeness."

Why Not Lost?

For a moment, put yourself in the shoes of a person who is not connected to Jesus. Assume that you are somewhat interested in discovering
more about the possibilities of developing a deeper relationship with
Him and that you might even be willing to associate with a church that
could facilitate your spiritual growth. After checking around, you identify a congregation that might be a good place to start your explorations.
To your satisfaction, you hear them describe your situation. To your hor-
ror, you hear them label you as "lost." In your mind, that is a demeaning,
arrogant and inaccurate term. It is also a word that reveals the heart of
the people who use it: They cannot be
loving or understanding if they elevate
themselves to a place of knowing what is
right while anyone who believes differently is inferior or lost.

The terms "non-Christian" and "non-believer" are rejected because most of the unchurched deem themselves to be Christian.

Does that sound far-fetched? It is
not. In fact, it describes a fairly common
scenario in which the unchurched misin-
terpret what we mean and depart from
the church with emotional bruises. In
our surveys we found that 56 percent of
the unchurched say that they find the term offensive; only 6 percent say
they would look favorably upon a church that describes them as lost.

In the Hunt

If not "lost," then what do the unchurched want to be called? We tested
seven terms. The two most acceptable are "inquirer" and "explorer," each
of which is embraced by about half of the unchurched. Even the widely
used term "seeker" is not as popular; only 4 out of 10 say they prefer it.

Expressions that fall into the offensive territory include "non-Christian," "prodigal," "lost" and "nonbeliever." The terms "non-Christian" and "nonbeliever" are rejected because most of these people deem themselves to be Christian; their rejection of the Church and their not having a real or growing relationship with Jesus Christ are seen as irrelevant to the issue.

Table 7.2
What Do the Unchurched Want to Be Called?

preferred term	like it	subgroups especially fond of this label
inquirer	52%	men; parents; Democrats
explorer	48	men
seeker	40	Midwesterners
non-Christian	20	liberals; never-been-married
prodigal	13	born-again Christians; blacks
lost	11	no single group
nonbeliever	10	college graduates

Do not overlook the tone of the two terms that were the most popular. "Inquirer" and "explorer" are words that suggest the person is still in the hunt, that they have not given up on faith or spiritual development, even though they may have given up on the local church. The low standing of "nonbeliever" is consistent with this drive to remain a player in the spiritual realm.

THE RIGHT TREATMENT

The unchurched have strong feelings about what they do and do not want to experience if they return to a church. The information in table 7.3 describes what they like and dislike. Understanding these attitudes can help us craft an intelligent and strategic approach to make church attendance the most positive adventure possible.

When asked about specifics, most of the unchurched say they prefer low-key actions. Three out of four would like to get a note in the mail from the pastor as an acknowledgment of their presence and a thank-you for coming. Three out of four would like to be given information about the church that they can read in their own place, on their own time. Three out of four said they would like the church to do nothing special or unusual for them while they are visiting; they simply want to see what it is like to be at the church without anyone creating an artificial response to their presence.

Three out of five said they would not mind if a church had a special reception for visitors—after the service—to welcome and get to know them. We have learned that they want this to be after the service so that they can figure out whether or not the reception is worth their time and make up their mind as to whether or not they would consider returning to the church. Three out of five were willing to field a telephone call from either the pastor or someone from the church—interestingly, it really does not make much difference to them—during the week after their visit, to thank them for attending and to answer any questions they might have.

Table 7.3
How the Unchurched Want to Be Treated at Church

Like this response?	Yes	No	Not Sure
received a thank-you note from the pastor during the week after the visit, thanking you for visiting and inviting you to return	78%	13%	10%
they gave you information about the church	72	16	8
they did not do anything special for you or treat you any differently than anyone else	76	17	7

Continued on next page

Like this response?	Yes	No	Not Sure
members of the church came to you after the service and individually greeted you because you were visiting	72	22	7
they held a reception after the church service for church members to welcome and get to know visitors	64	28	8
you received a telephone call from the pastor to thank you for visiting and to ask if you have any questions about the church	61	29	9
you received a telephone call from someone from the church, other than the pastor, to thank you for visiting and to ask if you have any questions about the church	61	32	7
during the offering or collection they mentioned that they did not expect visitors to give money, since that is the responsibility of the people who are members of the church	46	32	23
someone from the church, other than the pastor, visited your home during the week after your visit to drop off a small gift, such as a plate of cookies or a loaf of bread, to thank you for visiting their church	45	47	8
they offered you a free audio tape of the church service that you could get after the service	41	47	12

Continued on next page

Like this response?	Yes	No	Not Sure
they asked you to identify yourself during your visit, so that people would know you were a visitor	39	55	6
they asked you to wear a special visitor's name tag	35	57	8
the pastor visited your home during the week after your visit to the church	34	58	8
someone from the church, other than the pastor, visited your home during the week after your visit to the church	30	62	8

Less than half of the unchurched expressed interest in each of the remaining responses. Those responses included: knowing that they are not expected to donate during their visit; receiving a small gift at their home for having attended; identifying themselves as a visitor during their visit; wearing a special visitor's nametag; and being visited at home, by either the pastor or someone else from the church. Our interviews indicate that control is a major issue. The unchurched do not want people exerting control over them. In this regard, the gift brought to their home may seem like manipulation. Identifying themselves makes them a target of unnatural attention. The home visit is an invasion of their turf and ignores their busy schedule. (These people resist home visits that are *unrequested*; if they invite you to their home, that is a different story.)

Different segments of the unchurched responded more favorably than others to certain types of treatment. Adults under 35, for instance, resonate with mentioning that visitors are not expected to provide a financial gift during the offertory. The least educated people express the greatest interest in getting a telephone call from someone, getting a gift or being visited by the pastor. Adults with the highest levels of education are less interested than other people in wearing nametags, having a gift dropped off or receiving a gift delivered to their home by a church member. Residents of the West are much less interested than other people in wearing nametags and going to receptions after services. Although most of the unchurched people in the South agree that they do not want anything special to be done for them, they are less likely to say this than are people living elsewhere. Southerners, and especially black adults, are interested in a visit from the pastor.

Since we started tracking the movement of the unchurched in the 1980s, we have seen some significant shifts in how they want churches to treat them. Table 7.4 displays some of the pertinent transitions. Notice that there is less timidity among the unchurched these days about being identified during their visit or about being contacted afterward. This is attributable to two changes: the growing sense of disconnection and loneliness in America and the relational emphasis of the Baby Busters and Mosaics. Things have not gotten to the point where it is an "anything-goes" open invitation to communicate at will with them, but there is a definite loosening up of the restrictions they feel regarding being controlled.

Table 7.4
How Desired Treatment of the Unchurched Has Changed in the 1990s

	Like this response		
	2000	**1995**	**1990**
received a thank-you note from the pastor during the week after the visit, thanking you for visiting and inviting you to return	78%	70%	70%
they gave you information about the church	72	70	74
they did not do anything special for you or treat you any differently from anyone else	76	79	56

Continued on next page

	Like this response		
	2000	**1995**	**1990**
members of the church came to you after the service and individually greeted you because you were visiting	72	78	67
they held a reception after the church service for church members to welcome and get to know visitors	64	65	60
you received a telephone call from the pastor or someone else from the church to thank you for visiting and to ask if you have any questions about the church	61	60	63
someone from the church, other than the pastor, visited your home during the week after your visit to drop off a small gift, such as a plate of cookies or a loaf of bread, to thank you for visiting their church	45	22	NA
they asked you to identify yourself during your visit, so that people would know you were a visitor	39	22	23
they asked you to wear a special visitor's name tag	35	26	21
the pastor visited your home during the week after your visit to the church	34	33	34

EMPHASIS ON MINISTRY

The research also reminds us that different elements of ministry appeal to different types of people. We asked the unchurched what kind of church they would prefer, based upon the ministry emphasis of the church. Their answers were divided rather evenly among the four choices we provided. One-quarter prefer a church where the emphasis is on serving needy people in their area. One-quarter prefer a church with an evangelistic emphasis. One-fifth are most interested in a church that stresses teaching the Bible. One-sixth seek a place where the dominant emphasis is on building relationships, support and accountability among believers. The remaining one-eighth do not have any idea what type of church they want—but a large share of those people are individuals who are very unlikely to return to the Church (i.e., atheists and people with no interest in faith).

> A church that focuses on serving the needy is attractive to the most affluent of the unchurched.

Furthermore, questions about ministry emphasis help define specialized niches within the unchurched community. A majority of the born-again adults express an interest in an evangelistic congregation. A highly relational ministry is of comparatively greater interest to people living in the Northeast. A church that focuses on serving the needy is attractive to the most affluent of the unchurched, to people who are politically and socially liberal and to residents of the West.

THE IDEAL CHURCH

To further demonstrate the diversity of preferences among the unchurched, we asked them to make choices between 11 pairs of possibilities that pertain to what type of church they would ideally like to attend. There was only one factor for which even half of the unchurched indicated that they had a strong preference—and that was only 52 percent who said they would prefer a church of 200 people to a church of 1,000. There are almost as many combinations of preferences as there are unchurched people.

We did, however, find that there are a number of leanings that the unchurched possess. If the majority, or plurality, were to rule, churches would

- provide traditional music (including a choir and organ)
- feature topical sermons
- create an informal environment
- have fewer than 200 people
- include substantial participation in the service by everyone
- allow children to attend the services with their parents
- maintain a reserved and orderly service
- have time set aside within the service for people to pray for and minister to each other

Table 7.5
The Preferred Elements of a Church

	strongly	somewhat	total
OPTION A: service with traditional hymns or	26%	21%	47%
OPTION B: service with contemporary worship music	14	16	30
OPTION A: with a formal worship service	18	18	36
OPTION B: with an informal worship service	23	26	48
OPTION A: with less than 100 people attending	30	26	55
OPTION B: with more than 300 people attending	8	14	22

Continued on next page

	strongly	somewhat	total
OPTION A: with less than 200 people attending	52	24	77
OPTION B: with more than 1,000 people attending	3	3	7
OPTION A: service that has everyone participate throughout the service	33	20	53
OPTION B: service with little participation, where the people watch the leaders conduct the service	17	17	34
OPTION A: service in which children attend with their parents, and there is a section of the service geared to children	43	13	56
OPTION B: service just for adults, with children enrolled in classes that meet elsewhere during the adult service	23	10	33
OPTION A: with a choir that is accompanied by an organ	29	24	53
OPTION B: with a singer who leads the congregation in songs, accompanied by a band playing electric instruments	12	11	23
OPTION A: at which people raise their hands, applaud and make other verbal affirmations or noises during the musical portion of the worship service	18	13	31
OPTION B: at which people are reserved and orderly during the service	35	21	55

Continued on next page

	strongly	somewhat	total
OPTION A: at which Communion is offered as part of service	26	18	44
OPTION B: at which Communion is offered only at special services at other times of the year	17	17	34
OPTION A: at which time is set aside for people to pray with or minister to each other during the service	29	21	51
OPTION B: at which there is no interaction among people during the service, other than a brief greeting to those seated nearby	17	20	37
OPTION A: at which the sermons address issues or concerns that people face in their lives	44	19	62
OPTION B: at which the sermons are based on studying a specific book of the Bible, with a verse by verse explanation of those passages	15	6	21

Upon exploring various niches, though, divergent combinations of preferences were expressed. Each of these groups would create churches and church services that look and feel quite different. Here are a few examples of these combinations:

- People under 35 prefer a service that includes music—both traditional and contemporary—played by an electric band with a "worship leader." They want children to attend the services with their parents (perhaps because they feel they never received the nurture they wanted), and they would prefer that more than 300 people be at the services. Their ideal service would facilitate a lot of congregational participation and allow time for people in the congregation to minister to each other.

- People 50 and older prefer a service that features traditional hymns and unfolds in an orderly and reserved manner—no raising of hands, applauding or making noise during the service, and no children accompanying their parents. These older individuals do not want time set aside for interaction among congregants, other than the turn-and-greet routine. They also prefer services that require minimum participation.

- Black adults opt for services in which the entire family attends together, there is a high level of personal involvement and there is a high degree of expressiveness—clapping, shouting, applauding and the like. They prefer services in which time is included for people to pray with and minister to each other, as well as time set aside for communion.

- Whites, on the other hand, lean toward an informal service, but one that is more orderly and reserved.

- Adults in the South would create an informal atmosphere for congregations of 200 or fewer people. They would use contemporary worship music provided by an electric band with a music leader and seek substantial participation in the service by everyone present. Communion would be reserved for special services and events held throughout the year, but time would be included in each week's service for attendees to pray with and minister to each other.

- People in the upper income ranges also vied for an informal atmosphere and contemporary worship music. However, they also would want a service that required limited participation from people, reserved and orderly behavior, children shuffled off to classes and no time set aside to pray for and minister to others during the service. They, like most people, would like to be in a congregation of fewer than 200 people.

Some of the results of our research surprised us, particularly that such a large proportion of the unchurched feel more comfortable with traditional church music than with contemporary worship music. In fact, they prefer choirs and organs over guitars and drums. It was also a surprise to discover that they desire to have time within the service for interpersonal ministry and prefer congregations of 200 or fewer people. How does this fit?

Traditional church music not only appeals to most of the people 50 and older, but it also appeals to a stunning percentage of people under 35. One of the hallmarks of that group, of course, is their need for moorings in life, and within the church context that often means returning to music and traditions that give them greater cohesion and foundations in life. The unique twist among the young adults, though, is that they prefer that the old-time hymns be played by an electric band led by a worship leader and have a contemporary feel.

The desire for time to minister to each other is a reflection of the national trends toward greater participation in every event, people's desire for control over their environment, the drive toward increased lay ministry and the expanding sense of alienation and loneliness. Many people look at their church experience as an opportunity to address their need to take responsibility for the shaping and development of their life, including how they are ministered to and their own ability to be a help to others in spiritual matters.

The preference for smaller churches rather than megachurches is also surprising. In light of the unchurched's desire to remain somewhat anonymous during their initial visits to a service, we might have anticipated the unchurched to gravitate automatically toward larger congregations. However, they want smaller ones. A major reason goes back to their desire for personal connections. Their assumption is that they will have an easier time connecting with people, gaining some level of significance and finding a more welcoming atmosphere in a small church.

It seems that many unchurched people wind up returning to megachurches. Why? Because the people in those large bodies are more likely to invite outsiders to visit than the people in smaller ones. Many churches are small because the members are comfortable in a small body. Each time a newcomer visits, the security of the known is dissipated a bit, creating greater discomfort for them. In contrast, one of the

common expectations expressed to the people who attend larger churches is that they should invite their unchurched friends.

Large churches, in other words, become large because they strive to
become large; small churches remain small because they typically possess a small-church mentality. Thus,
even though most unchurched people
might prefer a small church, many of
them wind up at a large church. The
catalyst behind the leanings of a
church—that is, whether to remain
small or go for size—is leadership. Large
churches embrace the attitude of
growth because the church leadership
promotes that mind-set. In smaller churches, leadership often focuses
on internal ministry rather than external outreach.

> In smaller churches,
> leadership often
> focuses on internal
> ministry rather than
> external outreach.

THE KEY TO THE PROCESS

The information regarding what people want from a church once again
emphasizes that there are many different tastes, needs and expectations
among the unchurched. A church might be just what God intends it to
be, yet it may not be at all attractive to certain unchurched people—and
that is to be expected, given the "satisfy me with a customized experience" mind-set of a growing number of Americans.

Ultimately, the key to the process turns out to be the people in the
church. Outsiders visit a church looking for insiders who are sensitive to
the needs and background of the unchurched. They seek people who will
be flexible enough to adjust to some of those needs and whose
demeanor and behavior are stellar examples of authentic Christianity in
action. It used to be that unchurched people complained that churches
spent too much time and effort raising money from congregants. That
is no longer the issue today. The new point of irritation is the alleged
hypocrisy of the congregants.

In practical terms, a church would be better off to ensure that its
people live full Christian lives. Its members should be joyful and consis-

tent in their personal lives. And they should be eager to welcome new-comers into their family of faith. Only then should a church launch marketing efforts, program changes and special events designed to attract unchurched people. Events, programs and advertising might prompt a person to visit once, but if that person does not sense that the church is a place of internal consistency and overt love, he or she will not come back—either to that church or, often, to any other.

Think of it this way: Our responsibility is bigger than whether or not we grow numerically. Each time an unchurched individual visits a church and chooses not to return, his or her experience may well deter-mine his or her likelihood of ever returning to a Christian church. We cannot force an individual to stay, nor can we guarantee that our church will satisfy all of his or her needs. However, we can ensure that the unchurched visitor knows that our church is a dynamic and positive expression of what Jesus must have had in mind when He said that the gates of Hades would not overcome His Church (see Matt. 16:18).

WHICH OF THE FOLLOWING DID UNCHURCHED PEOPLE SAY IS THE MOST IMPORTANT FACTOR WHEN SELECTING A CHURCH?

A. The theological beliefs and doctrines
B. The quality of the programs and classes for children
C. How much the church is involved in helping the poor and disadvantaged
D. The quality of the sermons
E. Getting a personal invitation or recommendation from someone they know and trust
F. How much the people in the church seem to care about each other

CHAPTER 8

GRABBING THEIR ATTENTION

With the onslaught of technology in recent years, the number of methods that are available to convey tailored messages to the unchurched has grown considerably. Of course, not every method is amenable to the Church's mission and values, some methods are not cost-effective and not every message is compelling and appropriate.

A church's decision about the ways that it will reach out to unchurched people will have a tremendous impact upon its ability to minister successfully to the group. The message the church chooses to convey will position it in a positive, negative or indifferent way. The media used will gain an audience or simply drain a church's limited resources. These choices matter, just as the decision of how to minister to the unchurched once they visit the church or engage with its people is of vital importance.

The significance of remaining competitive in the marketplace cannot be overemphasized. These are not the "good ol' days" when people were meaningfully connected to a network of other people in their neighborhoods and at their workplaces. This is not the era when people knew the names of the churches in their communities and probably knew which church their neighbors attended. No longer do people look to churches to provide guidance on key moral and local issues. Churches, with amazing swiftness, are becoming the invisible institutions of our communities.

NAME THAT CHURCH

In a national survey among the unchurched, we found that only half of them (51 percent) claimed that they can remember the name of even one church within a 15-minute drive from their homes. We have also discovered that when people say they can recall such information, the chances are good that many of them cannot actually do so, which makes the statistic an overestimate of reality. We also know that many of the people who say they can name a local church identify places by generic or vague names: First Baptist, Lutheran, the Catholic Church and First Methodist are some common examples.

Furthermore, when we have the ability to check the church names that are provided to us against the names of existing churches in a particular area, fewer than one out of four unchurched adults can name at least one existing church. In fact, we discovered that only two out of every three unchurched people (65 percent) even know someone who attends a church in the area. This is a serious decline from the days when if a person did not attend church, he or she knew many people who did. The implication is that the chances of an unchurched person being invited to attend a church by someone who frequents one are diminishing.

The Unknown Denominations

The general awareness of religious institutions among Americans is also deteriorating. We asked a national sample of unchurched people to identify the names of religious institutions and denominations with which they were familiar. The results were amazing. The most frequently named denomination was Roman Catholic, mentioned by slightly more than half of the unchurched adults (56 percent). Next on the list were Baptist (34 percent), Jewish (22 percent), Christian (18 percent), Protestant (18 percent), Methodist (16 percent), Mormon (13 percent) and Lutheran (11 percent). No other denominations were named by at least 10 percent of the people surveyed.

Look at that list. At least one denomination was recalled by about half of the unchurched, only one more was remembered by at least one-quarter of the group and only two other Protestant denominations were identified by at least 1 out of 10 people. The Jewish synagogues of America, though serving just 2 percent of the population, were more likely to be recalled than were Methodist or Lutheran churches. Presbyterian churches were outpaced by Mormon churches. Jehovah's

Witness Kingdom Halls and Muslim mosques had greater recall levels than did Episcopalian churches. The Church of Christ, Assembly of God, Nazarene and Church of God denominations did not make the radar screen.

Not Like It Once Was

The point of this recitation is not to applaud some churches and denigrate others. Frankly, these recall levels are appallingly small for organizations that have been around for decades, have hundreds of franchises around the nation, represent churches that spend billions of dollars each year and have a mission that includes penetrating the community with their presence. The point is that Christian churches of every shape and form are losing their place in people's consciousness. There may have been a time in America's history when targeting a community and hanging a shingle would have been enough to attract a core group upon which the church could be founded and expanded. Today, denominational names and distinctions are meaningless to most people—unchurched and churched. Even knowing that there are a plethora of churches operating within the community is lost knowledge.

So what will it take to restore the unchurched's awareness of the church choices and distinctions that reside right under the their noses? Let's consider the information about a church that matters the most to them, the communications that influence their thinking and choices and the role of personal relationships in reaching the unchurched.

KEY FACTORS IN THEIR CHOICE

When unchurched people seek information about a church, they pay attention to certain bits of insight and ignore other facts. Often, the information that people in the church think would be important turns out to be irrelevant. Table 8.1 shows the priorities of the unchurched.

True Believers

As I noted in chapter 7, the unchurched look for evidence of real Christianity. To them, that is manifested in people within a church who truly love each other. Two-thirds said that is either extremely or very important to them when they evaluate whether or not they would like a church. Another indicator of value to them is the quality of the sermons. Importantly, they do not seek moral truth as much as they yearn for personal relevance and a loving tone. (Keep in mind that they are not likely to think of biblical truth as the core of relevance; the real issue is how that truth is conveyed. We dare not compromise God's truth and principles, but we are likely to gain an audience with the unchurched only if the manner in which we convey those insights seems reasonable, compassionate, contemporary and personally applicable.)

Theological Agreement

Six out of 10 unchurched people are also anxious to find a church that has theological beliefs and doctrinal stands that they deem palatable. Of course, when the unchurched talk about theology and doctrine, they do not get into the finer points of soteriology, eschatology or ecclesiology. Their scrutiny focuses on fundamental questions such as: Do you believe in a literal interpretation of the Bible? Do you believe that Jesus is God? What do you teach about forgiveness and eternity? Do you push tithing? What behaviors constitute sin in your system? In essence, they seek to figure out what part of the spiritual world a church and its leaders occupy: Protestantism, Catholicism, Eastern mysticism, metaphysical groups or something else. The finer points of theology are not at stake here; they simply want to understand the overall leanings.

> Unchurched adults are striving to identify the heart of the people in the congregation.

Six out of 10 are also very interested in being associated with a church that helps the poor and disadvantaged people in their community. Our work has shown that unchurched adults are striving to identify the heart of the people in the congregation more than they are seeking out opportunities to get involved personally. Again, their objective is to discover evidence of the authenticity of the people's faith commitment.

The Importance of Programs

About half of the unchurched said that the emphasis on children having quality programs and classes is of great importance to them. Among the unchurched who actually have children under 18, this was the single most important item of all: seven out of 10 rated it as either "extremely" or "very" important. Among unchurched adults who do not have children, this was one of the lowest-rated factors tested.

Let's pause here for a moment. Realize that of the dozen factors we tested, these were the only ones that at least half of the unchurched said were important to them. Keep in mind, of course, that there was no "cost" to the unchurched person associated with saying that any of these factors were critically important. Consequently, the fact that the other items on the list were not deemed highly significant is in itself highly significant.

Of Lesser Value

The items that were comparatively less important included being personally impressed by someone they know who attends the church; the quality of the church's worship music; a personal invitation or recommendation from someone they know; the denominational affiliation of the church; the distance of the church from their home; the evangelistic fervor of the congregation; and the church's degree of political action.

Changing Times

Upon comparing the current findings with those from past years, we find a few patterns that can be explained by related insights into current cultural change. For instance, although a church's theology and doctrine remain quite important to people, the relative importance of that content has declined substantially in the past decade. This fits with the trend of homogenized theology and substantive tolerance: It does not matter what a person believes as long as he or she believes something, and it is more important for a person to be accepting of others' views than to be right. In an environment in which there is no absolute moral truth, the existence of belief transcends the importance of the substance of those beliefs.

Denominational affiliation is also less important to people than it was in 1990—and even then it was less significant to people than it had been two decades earlier. This, too, fits the trend in our culture: People matter, institutions do not. As Americans assess who they are, who they want to be and how they wish to be perceived by others, the chances of them shaping their character and image to integrate the values and nature of a macro-level institution, such as a denomination, are declining. We have noticed during the 1990s that fewer and fewer people describe themselves as Presbyterian, Lutheran or Methodist, for instance, but instead simply say they are Christian, Protestant or spiritual.

Table 8.1
The Importance of Different Factors to the Unchurched When They Select a Church to Visit

	— how important is this factor? —				
	ex-tremely	very	only somewhat	not too	not at all
how much the people in the church seem to care about each other	46%	20%	22%	4%	9%
the quality of the sermons	42	23	17	5	12
their theological beliefs and doctrine	41	20	19	6	11
how much the church is involved in helping the poor and disadvantaged	38	22	25	5	9
the quality of programs and classes for children	36	18	18	9	18

Continued on next page

	— how important is this factor? —				
	ex- tremely	very	only somewhat	not too	not at all
your impressions of the people you know who attend the church	19	20	30	12	17
the quality of the music in the services	19	18	28	12	23
denominational affiliation of the church	18	17	29	12	20
how committed the people in the church are to sharing their faith	15	10	29	15	29
a personal invitation or recommendation from someone you know and trust	14	22	31	14	17
how far the church is from your home	14	18	31	10	25
how much the church is involved in political and social issues	14	10	21	13	38

The mobility and adventuresome spirit of Americans has led to making factors such as the distance of a church from home less important. Today people will drive as far as they have to drive in order to have a good experience. It may be a relational experience, a spiritual experience, an entertainment experience or an intellectual experience, but experience rules in our culture. If it takes an extra few minutes or dollars to gain access to a superior experience, we tend to deem it to be worthwhile.

Cut Through the Clutter

Communications analysts estimate that the typical American is exposed to an average of 1,500 to 2,000 commercial and promotional messages every day. We are bombarded with commercials everywhere we turn: on license plate holders, coffee mugs, pens, the sides of trucks and the first few minutes of movie rentals. We even see them in church bulletins. Anything that has public visibility is a potential ad space. The profusion of ads has made the ability to slice through the clutter a daunting challenge to modern communicators and marketers.

The typical church has a minimal budget for advertising and limited expertise in such forms of communication. How can churches hope to cut through the clutter to reach their desired audience and to hit home with a precise and compelling message? The answer lies partially in knowing how to target those communication efforts.

Advertising That Works

Table 8.2 points out that only three out of the nine methods tested seem to have much pull with the unchurched—and all three of those methods depend on personal relationships. The greatest influence is a personal invitation from a friend. Two-thirds of the unchurched said that such an overture would have a positive effect on them. Notice that only one out of every 25 unchurched adults said that if they were invited to attend a church, it would make them *less* likely to do so. We know from the earlier observations mentioned in this book that unchurched people are less likely than churched people to be highly relational in nature. Even so, they are affected by the personal touch, especially when it comes from a friend whose judgment and sensitivity they trust.

A Personal Touch

A personal invitation from a pastor has almost as great an impact. Even though it may be an expected, professional gesture, people are likely to react in a positive manner. This approach is significant particularly to Busters, who generally feel snubbed or undervalued by people in positions of authority or by older people, and to blacks, who still tend to regard pastors as the leaders of the black community and as individuals worthy of respect.

Believers ought to be careful regarding the things they say about their church when they are in public. The surveys we conducted show that one of the most powerful influences on an unchurched person's behavior is what they hear from their friends about the life of a church. We also discovered that when churched people talk about significant changes made at a church to make its ministry more relevant, almost half of the unchurched people exposed to such conversation are more likely to consider attending that church.

Traditional Marketing

Two things must be noted about the use of traditional marketing methods, such as print advertising, broadcasting, telemarketing and direct mail. First, in most cases none of those approaches has enough impact to justify the costs involved. The people most likely to be attentive to such communications are already churched, which means that if the message is successful in bringing people to the church being promoted, all it has done is steal people from other churches. Meanwhile, the unchurched—the real target audience—pay little attention.

Second, when we compare the ability of these media to reach the unchurched to their ability to do so a decade ago, a huge change has taken place. In 1990, the unchurched were active consumers of such contacts, although not always for the better (i.e., some church media efforts actually made them less likely to attend the church). The big issue today is widespread indifference to communications. As table 8.2 reveals, the dominant reaction to most church-based communication efforts is ambivalence. In 1990, people were likely to be incensed by a telephone call from a telemarketer on behalf of a church. Times have changed. Today, they are more likely to hang up immediately (if the call even penetrates their call screening or answering machine) without giving it a second thought. Ten years ago, consumers scrutinized every piece of mail that came their way, even overt junk mail. Today, a growing number of pieces of mail never get to the "opened" stage, much less to the "read before discarded" stage. Making an impression on consumers is much more difficult than it was a decade or so ago. The methods that work best are those that are most personal.

Table 8.2
Prime Media for Marketing the Church (impact of communication methods on the likelihood of attending a church)

	impact upon likelihood of attending a church:			
	a lot more	little more	makes difference	no less
invited by a friend or neighbor	27%	36%	32%	4%
invited by the pastor	22	28	40	6
heard good things about the church from a friend	21	27	47	4
received a telephone call inviting you to attend	8	19	49	21
saw or heard a broadcast of the church's worship services	7	14	60	16
received a mailed flyer/brochure	6	14	61	18
saw a television ad for the church	5	11	63	20
church name sounds appealing	4	7	77	10
saw an ad for the church in the newspaper or Yellow Pages	3	6	74	16

Name Recognition

Some churches have tried to expand and exploit the name recognition of their senior pastor as a means of building the church's congregation. The assumption is that because he or she has prayed at local events, has sent mailers to households throughout the community and has served on community task forces, people will know and respect the pastor. Involvement in those types of activities might have built a high profile for a pastor in the 1950s, but times have changed. No matter how well known and highly respected church members think their pastor is, chances are good that most of the people in the area are not aware of him or her. Here are several illustrations of that concept.

Most people who will read this book know of Beverly LaHaye, Josh McDowell, Gary Smalley and Charles Swindoll. Each of them has had extensive media ministries and has written best-selling books. They have been newsmakers for years and have spoken to thousands upon thousands of people. Born-again Christians all over America are familiar with their names, their faces and their ministry efforts. But not one of them is known to even 1 out of every 20 unchurched adults.

The pastor of one of the largest and best-known churches in America is Bill Hybels of Willow Creek Community Church outside of Chicago. Hybels has authored books that have topped the charts as Christian best-sellers. Audiotapes of his sermons sell by the thousands. The conferences held at Willow Creek each year, featuring Hybels and other speakers, sell out within weeks of being announced. He has been a counselor to the president of the United States and has started an international association of "seeker" churches. He has been called the most influential pastor in America. Hybels is known by fewer than 1 out of 4 churched people and by less than 3 percent of the unchurched.

Dr. James Dobson has been hosting the *Focus on the Family* program for more than a quarter century. His show is heard on more than 1,500 radio stations every day. His books and videos have sold millions of copies. He has faithfully served presidents, congressional committees and national family-policy study groups. His organization is visited by tens of thousands of people every year and contacted by hundreds of thousands. The variety of magazines they produce for targeted audiences—including adolescents, teenagers, parents, pastors, doctors, teachers and grandparents—are read by millions of families and individuals. He has appeared on national news and talk programs and has been featured in numerous national news stories about Christian perspectives on current issues. When Christian marketers want to get the endorsement of a highly respected, well-known Christian figure, Dr. Dobson is one of the names high on the list. And yet fewer than one out of every five unchurched adults have ever heard of Dr. James Dobson.

Using individuals from a church, such as a pastor or other local celebrities, to raise people's awareness of and interest in a church is a difficult strategy to employ successfully. Church leaders should think twice before they embark on this path. Few have used it to their advantage. If the unchurched do not know these national figures, what are the chances they will know a local pastor who has much lower visibility and fewer opportunities to get exposure among local residents?

POSITIONING THE CHURCH

The choice of messages that a church delivers to its target audience also makes a difference in its ability to affect people's attitudes and behavior. The choices are seemingly endless, but our limited evaluation of even a few, simple positioning points shows the importance of a church's leaders knowing how they want to be perceived and effectively conveying information that fosters that image.

Consistent with other findings from our research, we discovered that of the seven descriptions tested, the approach that appeals the most to the unchurched is an active involvement in helping poor and disadvantaged people. Half of the unchurched said that this type of positioning makes a church "very appealing," and another one-third said it makes a church "somewhat appealing." This image is especially appealing to women, downscale individuals and black adults.

The next most attractive positioning is to communicate that the church is meeting the needs of the entire family unit. About two out of five adults said this makes a church "very appealing," and one-third said it makes the church "somewhat appealing." Nearly identical results were obtained when we asked about positioning a church as concerned about the declining morals in American society.

Being known as a place that helps people apply Christianity to their daily lives was slightly less appealing to people, but it still drew positive reaction from a majority. Lesser appeal was associated with being positioned as a church that is "relevant for your life today" or being "biblically based." By far the least appealing image was being a church that is politically active. Only 1 out of 10 adults said that such an image made the church "very appealing," and 2 out of 10 stated that such a church would be "somewhat appealing" to them. Most significantly, half of the unchurched said that a church that prides itself on being politically active would be "not at all appealing" to them.

Various niches within the unchurched population expressed atypical preferences. For instance, Builders (people in their mid-50s to early 70s) were more likely to be drawn to a church that is said to be biblically based, concerned about moral decline and focused on applicable Christianity. The skepticism of wealthy people (i.e., people with college degrees and above-average incomes) was evident: Across the board they were less likely than were other adults to say that any of these positioning statements makes a church more appealing. Black adults are especially influenced by hearing that a church is helping the needy and that it seeks to facilitate faith applications.

EXPLOITING THE OPPORTUNITIES

Without a doubt, one of the most important strategies to employ in influencing the unchurched is to have their trusted friends invite them to attend church. This is not a new idea. For at least a half century, proponents of church growth have described the significance of friendship evangelism, personal relationships and marketing through word of mouth.

How are we doing at following through on this known principle? According to the unchurched, 1 out of 4 of them has been asked to attend a church service or church event with a friend in the past 12 months. Of those, 1 out of every 7 attended. In other words, if we look at the aggregate body of unchurched adults, 4 percent were invited to attend church with a friend and did so; 23 percent were invited to attend but declined; and 73 percent were never invited. What does this tell us?

Perhaps the most obvious observation is that most unchurched people are not being pursued by anyone. We outnumber them two to one. We are called by God to pursue them. We spend more than $3 billion every year in America constructing or renovating church facilities in which to host them. But the single most effective strategy of all—following Jesus' lead of asking them to "come and see"—is generally neglected.

FEW ARE ASKED TO ATTEND, EVEN FEWER COME

How Many Unchurched Were Personally Invited to a Church—and Attended—in the Past 12 Months?

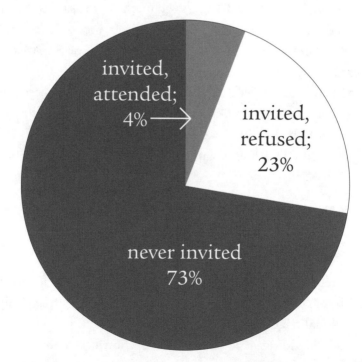

A second observation is that we have to be prepared for rejection. Almost 9 out of 10 unchurched people who were invited refused to go. But things may not be quite this bleak. Realize that we were interviewing the unchurched. What about the formerly unchurched who were invited, attended and have since remained connected to the life of a church? We do not have figures on the size of that group, but it would reduce the rejection statistics by some margin. Even so, rejection is a very real possibility when we attempt to lead a friend back to the church. That is simply a part of the game; we cannot let it deter us from engaging them and seeking to help them enjoy church life.

WHAT THEY NEED TO SEE

Some things never change. One of those things seems to be the ways by which unchurched people make their way back to the church. As much as at any time in the last 15 years or so, the key to drawing them back remains relationships and invitations. *They do not come if we do not ask.*

The unchurched have been there, done that, heard it all. In most cases, they are not going to be drawn to a church because of the size of the congregation, its history, the genius of the pastor, the talent of the musicians or the convenience of freeway access. Those things do not hurt, but they are not what rings the bells of the unchurched. They need to see a group of people who care about each other and those in need. They need to sense the relevance of the church— but it must be conveyed by example, not by proclamation of being relevant. And there must be something different about the church. The message and the experience, then, must be compelling, convincing and consistent. Anything less gets lost in the cacophony of self-promotional noise that we endure day in and day out.

> As much as at any time in the last 15 years or so, the key to drawing the unchurched back remains relationships.

How ironic it is that in this age of complexity, it is the simplest of strategies—asking someone to attend—that has the greatest power. However, our research highlights a harsh reality about the process of inviting the unchurched to accompany us to church: They will usually reject our offer. Perhaps the most intriguing reality is that they are rarely offended by a reasonable, well-intentioned request. Therefore, it may take us several attempts at bringing them to a church before they are ready to do so. We can neither be shy nor lack perseverance. While those offers must be made sensibly and sensitively, as people see things in us and hear things about our churches that are attractive, the odds of them accompanying us become better. Remember, as I already noted, in their eyes, attending a worship service is rarely the ideal initial introduction to a church.

As we discuss our church history and relationship with unchurched friends, bear in mind that they are more interested in having a positive experience than in learning accurate Bible content. The latter may be a highly defensible reason for pursuing them; the former may be the most plausible means of reaching them. Striking a viable balance is part of the art of influencing the unchurched to give Christianity and the Church another try.

Although the research clearly shows that most unchurched people do not go to church because of a radio commercial, mailed brochure or newspaper ad—and there are ample numbers of churches across America whose experience verifies this—the mass media may still be a useful weapon in your marketing arsenal. If the media can be used to support other outreach efforts—that is, as a secondary rather than a primary thrust—then it may justify its cost. A recent craze in advertising circles has been to achieve "message integration," meaning that the product or service advertised is supported by a multifaceted campaign in which all of the communications vehicles utilized are integrated in message, tone, offer and measurement. The notion of weaving together all of your church's efforts to penetrate the unchurched bears further consideration.

CHURCHES THAT HAVE BEEN SUCCESSFUL IN REACHING OUT TO THE UNCHURCHED DO WHICH OF THE FOLLOWING?

(THERE MAY BE MORE THAN ONE CORRECT ANSWER)

A. Follow the Saddleback and Willow Creek models
B. Host large-scale special events
C. Have a laity that is committed to the vision of reaching the unchurched
D. Have large, paid staffs
E. Have a pastor with a charismatic personality
F. Allow visitors to be anonymous

CHAPTER 9

TWELVE MISCONCEPTIONS ABOUT MINISTRY TO THE UNCHURCHED

One of the most interesting facets of the research we conduct is the ability to distinguish fact from fiction about particular aspects of ministry. Often, as we research a topic, we discover that there are myths believed by substantial numbers of people. Not surprisingly, as we evaluated the philosophy, process and ministry results of the churches that are unusually effective at ministering to the unchurched, we found a number of inconsistencies between what many people believe about reaching the unchurched and what really works. Because the acceptance of such myths can undermine the ability to have a positive impact in people's lives, in this chapter I will identify 12 common misconceptions regarding ministering to the unchurched. Hopefully, awareness of these false beliefs will lead to the elimination of incorrect thinking and ineffective practices, thereby improving the quality of future outreach efforts.

MISCONCEPTION #1:
SUCCESSFUL MINISTRY TO THE UNCHURCHED DEPENDS ON FOLLOWING THE RIGHT MODEL

Our national surveys among pastors indicate that most of them have a program or formulaic mentality about evangelism. Their notion is that reaching unchurched people and affecting their lives is no different than any other program: Identify the niche, develop a needs-solving activity, systematize it and then move the participants to the next level of spiritual maturity.

Our studies of the churches that do stellar work among the unchurched revealed a completely different mind-set. We found that this type of ministry is about developing a servant-minded culture within the church, not simply instituting an outreach program. Evangelism is not an activity but a lifestyle in these churches. For that lifestyle to be embraced by the congregation, it must be modeled by the pastoral staff and lay leaders for everyone to see and appreciate. We saw that if a church wants to be truly evangelistic and attract unchurched people, it must do more than have a contemporary worship service or change the language it uses to exorcise the Elizabethan terms and insider lingo that baffle the unchurched. It must change the hearts of its own people so that they become passionate about reaching people who have no connection with Christ. That transformation has little to do with choosing the Willow Creek model, the Saddleback model and any other program.

MISCONCEPTION #2:
DEALING WITH THE ATTITUDES OF THE UNCHURCHED TOWARD THE CHURCH AND CHRISTIANITY IS A BIG PROBLEM

Many pastors and believers assume that the toughest element in reaching the unchurched is changing their perceptions and attitudes about the Christian faith and the value of church. Often, we assume that nonchurchgoers possess contempt for the church and are stubborn in their refusal to see anything good about Christianity.

The pastors of the model churches we studied have arrived at a different conclusion. The people with the attitude problem, according to successful pastors, are more likely to be the churched Christians. Granted, there is a contingent of unchurched people who cannot force themselves to think a civil thought about Christianity or the Church. But they are not going to set foot in a sanctuary anyway. The millions of unchurched individuals who do return to church to check it out are usually more open-minded and malleable than we think. The more audacious task is getting churched people genuinely to care about the souls and lives of those visitors. Congregation members balk at giving up their close-to-the-door parking spaces. They just cannot seem to find the time to get to know the newcomers. They refuse to ante up the money it takes to cover the costs of reaching out to the unchurched. They show little, if any, excitement about a church that is not necessarily designed exclusively to meet their personal needs. It is one thing to talk about the importance of capturing the hearts of wayward sinners for Christ, but it is another thing altogether to make the sacrifices necessary to accomplish that end.

MISCONCEPTION #3:
YOU MUST HAVE A SEEKER SERVICE

Willow Creek Community Church in South Barrington, Illinois, popularized the notion of having a weekend service that is specifically designed to attract and help unchurched people rather than one for believers that is focused on worship. The Willow Creek model contains some elements of a typical worship service—most notably prayer, music and a teaching time. However, these have been refined to eliminate the expectation that an unchurched person would worship a God that he or she does not know. Instead, the service is developed to expose that person to the relevance of the Bible, to positive thoughts about Christianity, to the friendliness of church people and to an environment in which the unchurched feel welcome, comfortable and helped.

In our sample of the congregations most effective at reaching the unchurched, few offer a seeker service. Most, however, provide full-on worship services that have been cleansed of Christian jargon, pipe organs, formal dress and traditional symbols, although the latter seems to be making a comeback, given the predispositions of Busters and Mosaics to seek spiritual moorings from ancient traditions and practices. These are churches that want unchurched people to be in a place of worship while worship is happening. "There has to be a place for someone who is skeptical or unconvinced to see and experience Jesus for who He is. And the best place for that is in the context of corporate worship," one young pastor said. His church has grown from zero to 2,000 adults in seven years; almost two-thirds of them were unchurched at the time they first visited that church. "To us, there's something about not only God's presence being there, but also the community functioning in love and faith, that allows someone to encounter Jesus in a way that he or she is probably not going to encounter Him elsewhere."

A number of the pastors indicated that their services are seeker sensitive, not seeker driven. "What we do may seem like it was designed for seekers, but it was not. Believers live in the same world as the unchurched, so the style of music and communication that connect well with the followers of Christ are likely to connect with those who are not yet following Him, too. The sensitivity to unchurched people is more likely to emerge in other ways." This midwestern pastor of a midsized church named the ways in which the greeting, follow-up, child care, parking and post-service interaction are handled as examples of how they fine-tune the process to incorporate the unchurched.

MISCONCEPTION #4:
THE BEST WAY TO ATTRACT THE UNCHURCHED IS THROUGH LARGE-SCALE EVENTS

About half of the model churches we studied use large-scale events to attract unchurched people. However, about half of those churches use them to build name awareness, develop relational bridges and create an image for their church. Only a couple of the effective churches we studied rely upon events to bring about change in the lives of the unchurched. Relatively few expect most of the individuals who attend the event to show up in church next Sunday. "We're establishing our presence, that's all," was how a pastor from a growing Baptist church in the South put it. "I can't reach them with radio or TV, but if I can give them a good time at a pleasant event, they'll remember us next time a friend mentions our church or next time they pass our building. If they meet some good people and sense that we're really part of the community, not just a bunch of religious fanatics out to take away their fun and impose a bunch of rules, then we might have a shot at seeing them visit our church sometime—when they're ready."

Surprisingly, a number of the effective churches do not use events at all. One of the largest churches in Ohio, built primarily on reaching the unchurched, indicated that events are counterproductive to what they hope to achieve. "We're trying to create an approach of evangelism as a lifestyle. If we suddenly start relying on events, we send the wrong message to our people. Instead, we encourage people-building relationships, not handing out tickets to events, no matter how good the event may be." Another pastor admitted that he sends people to the events put on by other churches. "It's not what we do. We're into building God's kingdom, so I don't need to have my own Easter show and Christmas special. If the church down the street does a great job at it, let's encourage people to take advantage of what they're doing. We have to focus on what makes us tick, and that's getting to know people and ministering on a one-to-one level."

MISCONCEPTION #5:
THE ROUTE TO SUCCESS IS TO COPY WILLOW CREEK OR SADDLEBACK

Most of the model churches we surveyed are very familiar with the work of two ground-breaking churches, Saddleback Church in Lake Forest, California, and Willow Creek. But not one church leader said that he uses either as a model. "We're pretty eclectic," laughed a pastor from California. "We steal from everybody. Willow [Creek] has some great stuff, and we've adapted a few things from them. Saddleback has some wonderful ideas, too, and we've ripped off a few things from them. But we read a lot, we talk to our visitors, we're out in the community, we go to conferences—there's no single source of insight on this stuff for us."

While these church leaders revere pioneers such as Bill Hybels at Willow Creek and Rick Warren at Saddleback, they also recognize the limitations of blindly copying what has worked in other places. The principles and materials developed by the two giant churches are studied and adapted. The flattery by imitation stops at that point.

MISCONCEPTION #6:
IF YOU DO IT RIGHT, MOST OF THE PEOPLE IN YOUR CHURCH WILL HAVE BEEN UNCHURCHED BEFORE THEY CHOSE YOURS AS THEIR HOME CHURCH

Nationwide, less than 20 percent of all church growth comes through conversion—that is, through people who were previously not followers of Christ but then accept Jesus as their savior and commit to involvement in a church. For most churches, numerical growth comes via births to members or transfers from other churches. Although the proportion of growth attributable to reaching the unchurched is much higher at churches that best reach and keep the unchurched, even in most of those places a majority of the growth is not attributable to reaching outsiders. Among the great churches we identified and studied vis-à-vis their ministry to the unchurched, the average number of current attendees who were previously unchurched was in the 40 to 50 percent range.

My intent is not to criticize that statistic. When we study this process and the people we hope to reach and think about getting almost half of our people from the pool of Americans who are living apart from the organized faith world, we stand in awe of churches that can attract such substantial numbers of irreligious people. But we must also see that even under the best of circumstances—which would be a church with leaders who are passionate about reaching the unchurched, a culture that facilitates reaching them and a ministry that is focused on attracting and retaining them—a majority of the people who adopt a church as their own will come from other churches.

For what it is worth, this is not all bad. As our interviews with the pastors and leaders of the effective churches highlighted indicate, every church needs an army of believers who grasp the vision of penetrating the unchurched population and are willing to make it their life's mission. Some of the church leaders we spoke to have been thwarted in their determination to attract the unchurched. But it is neither a lack of pastoral leadership or vision nor too small a pool of unchurched people from whom to draw that keeps them from reaching their goal. Rather, they have been handcuffed by the absence of enough believers who

> Nationwide, less than 20 percent of all church growth comes through conversion.

are excited about such a ministry. If new members at a church understand the vision of reaching the unchurched and those newcomers want to sign on for that purpose, then the leaders of that church gain a key resource—human capital—necessary to get the job done.

MISCONCEPTION #7:
IF YOU DO A GOOD JOB, MOST OF YOUR UNCHURCHED VISITORS WILL RETURN

We all hate rejection. Our natural reaction to being snubbed is to take it personally and to wonder what is wrong with us that caused another person to choose a behavior or lifestyle other than those that we have adopted and have made accessible to them. When a person visits our church but does not return, most of us interpret that as failure. His or her refusal to come back is viewed as a sign that we are doing something wrong.

At Barna Research, our evaluation of the model churches showed not only that they reach the unchurched, but also that they are effective at retaining them. Yet even in these churches a majority of the unchurched who visit will not ultimately stay. The range of unchurched visitors who did *not* return was from 30 to 70 percent; on average, about half come only once or a few times and then vanish. In many of the best-practices churches, we found that the majority of unchurched people who visit do not adopt the church as part of their life.

When we consider that these results come from the most effective churches, it certainly feels like Christianity has a relatively high rejection rate. The lesson in these numbers, though, is that not everyone who tries a church is going to feel comfortable there and choose it as his or her spiritual touchstone. The decision not to embrace a particular church does not necessarily mean the members and leadership have failed in their mission. We are striving to get the unchurched to make a major transition in their thinking and behavior. Change may be the defining characteristic of our culture, but it still comes with great struggle to the individuals within our culture. If we want to succeed in reaching the unchurched, the sad fact is that growth is, in crass terms, a numbers game. Even in response to our best efforts, some will walk away unconvinced. Having a tender heart and a tough skin are two necessary tools to begin and sustain this type of outreach.

MISCONCEPTION #8:
MINISTRY TO THE UNCHURCHED REQUIRES A LARGE STAFF

Several of the most effective churches started out by trying to increase the size of their staffs in order to handle the needs of a large number of unchurched people. Most of them eventually gave up this approach once they realized that the only way to be successful in ministering to significant numbers of unchurched people is to have the lay members of the congregation assume ministry roles. One pastor observed, "We found out that we just could not raise enough money to pull it off because when this is working, a large percentage of your congregation is unchurched and they do not give much money and they consume a huge amount of resources. Our only hope was to improve the servant attitude and activity of the members."

This pastor went on to describe the struggle of finding the proper balance between hiring paid professionals to do ministry and equipping the laity. Ultimately, a church that is serious about reaching unchurched people may wish to have an individual on staff whose primary function is strategizing, organizing and supervising the efforts to reach that target group. However, most of the churches we studied did not worry about having unique staff positions dedicated to unchurched ministry. "Our culture focuses on bringing unchurched people into our family. That's everyone's responsibility, within the context of every ministry function that takes place here," an associate pastor told us. "Everyone on staff is always conscious of the needs of the unchurched when they conceive and carry out their ministry. We don't have a 'pastor to the unchurched' because we all carry that as a subfunction or subconscious emphasis within our dominant frame of ministry—you know, discipleship, worship or whatever."

MISCONCEPTION #9:
THE UNCHURCHED REQUIRE ANONYMITY. WHEN THEY ARE READY TO GET INVOLVED, THEY WILL TELL YOU

My reason for including this notion in the "misconceptions" category is not because it is wrong. The unchurched usually do want to be anonymous. When they are ready to make a deeper commitment, they will let us know. They do not want to feel coerced into anything. However, I was surprised at how aggressive the effective churches are at facilitating a commitment among the unchurched.

Frankly, everything hinges on the unchurched person's willingness to identify himself or herself, usually by filling out a visitor's communication card during a service. Once that contact information is provided, the church springs into action, employing an intentional and strategic process designed to inform, encourage and motivate the visitor to move forward in the spiritual quest. This process, as I have already noted, usually includes a series of letters and postcards, one or two telephone calls and an invitation to attend a one- or two-session class for newcomers.

The key to success is not the actual steps taken but the tone of the communications. These churches do not engage in an insensitive play for warm bodies, but an energetic effort to let unchurched individuals know what is available to them and the process and implications of making a deeper commitment. These churches do not push the person into a commitment. Some tried that but realized that such an approach quickly raises the defenses or fears of the unchurched. For the unchurched individual, it is important to remain in control, at least in his or her mind. Pastors and the laity simply let the person know that the church cares, the church has ministries of value and there is an easy and minimally threatening process by which they can get into the mainstream of the church.

> For the unchurched individual, it is important to remain in control, at least in his or her mind.

MISCONCEPTION #10:
IF AN UNCHURCHED PERSON COMES FIVE OR SIX TIMES, HE OR SHE WILL STAY FOR GOOD

When a person comes a half dozen times to a church, it demonstrates continued interest and the willingness to change his or her existing behavioral patterns. So reaching the conclusion that the individual will stay makes sense. Unfortunately, even if an unchurched person comes to a church five or six times, he or she is not necessarily sold on what that church is all about.

The key is to go beyond having people attend and observe to having them attend and *get involved*. Once a person finds a point of connection—

a class or program to attend, a means of serving, a new friend—then he or she is more likely to feel like a part of the church. The bottom line is being connected—there must be relationship. Unless the newcomer is woven into a tapestry of meaningful or satisfying relationships, it is not unusual for him or her to come to worship services six, seven or more times and then disappear. Typically, an unchurched person who identifies a fulfilling activity undertaken in the company of likeable people in his or her first or second visit is more likely to remain in the church than a person who attends seven or eight times but is not interpersonally connected.

MISCONCEPTION #11:
SUCCESS IN REACHING
THE UNCHURCHED DEPENDS UPON THE PASTOR'S
PERSONALITY AND PREACHING

If we want to attract unchurched people to our church, it helps if the pastor has a charismatic personality and delivers clear and stirring sermons on topics of interest, with practical applications. But that is rarely enough to attract and retain the unchurched.

As I have already noted, according to the successful leaders we interviewed, the environment of the church and the attitude and spiritual commitment of the congregants are more important than the pastor and the preaching. "You can't really fool people into thinking you care if you don't," one pastor told us. "They've seen that a hundred times before. They're really sensitive to it."

Becoming part of a church is about developing an entirely new network of relationships and emotional connections. That's a big step for people; they move into it with caution, especially those who have been disappointed by churches in the past.

"It took me a while, but I realized that I could stand up there and preach heresy for weeks on end and they [the unchurched] either wouldn't care or didn't know the difference," said a pastor of a growing church in the Midwest. "What they *did* notice was how the people treated each other, how comfortable they felt in our place and what their kids said about their experience. They didn't want a lot of generic religious platitudes. Really, they weren't sure what they were looking for, but they'd experienced what they knew they *weren't* looking for. I'm not saying that preaching doesn't matter, but only that to the unchurched it doesn't matter as much as some of the other things they experience."

As I have already noted, most pastors at the model churches agreed that success comes not so much from their preaching or programs as from the actions of the Holy Spirit.

MISCONCEPTION #12:
ONCE YOU START ATTRACTING THE UNCHURCHED, THE CHALLENGE IS SIMPLY MANAGING THE FLOW OF INCOMING PEOPLE

Many pastors seem to believe that once you tap into the unchurched population, the word gets out and there is no stopping them from coming. Then the challenge becomes management rather than marketing.

Pastors in our sample said there is definitely some momentum that is generated once you begin to attract unchurched people, but there is no guarantee that such people will continue to stream into the church. "It's not like the unchurched are a community, or anything," laughed one pastor serving an evangelical church in the Southwest. "You have to stick to the fundamentals that got some of them coming in the first place."

The bigger issue, according to most of these church leaders, is not managing the newcomers but raising the resources to keep the ministry going. "I have an awfully tough time trying to find enough mature believers to mentor or teach or serve newcomers. Coming into this I knew that it would be tough to balance the resource mix—and even then, I really underestimated what it takes," said a pastor whose church grew by 1,000 people in less than three years, placing an incredible strain on the ministry. "But that's why we started this thing—we wanted to reach those people. Our problem is how to take proper care of them when they get here. And that's an issue with the churched people, not the unchurched. What happens when God answers our prayers and the unchurched come—and come and come and come? That's when it's time for believers to really step up to the plate and get the job done. That's what puts your heart to the test: Are you really willing to do what it takes to guide these people to the next step?"

A QUESTION TO PONDER

Obviously, ministry to the unchurched is a bit different from what you might have assumed. Are any of these misconceptions evident in your ministry?

PASTORS CITED WHICH OF THE FOLLOWING AS SIGNS THAT THEIR CHURCH WAS SUCCESSFULLY REACHING OUT TO THE UNCHURCHED?

(THERE IS MORE THAN ONE
CORRECT ANSWER)

A. Greater knowledge of basic Christian principles
B. More baptisms
C. Increased number of people in small groups
D. People indicating they have accepted Christ as their Savior
E. More church members inviting the unchurched to come to church
F. A high percentage of new members who have not joined by transfer

CHAPTER 10

How Churches Minister Effectively to the Unchurched

In this chapter I will share more key insights gleaned from our research into churches that have successfully reached the unchurched. But first let me set the stage for understanding how and why these churches are so effective.

It is helpful to understand that all of these model churches have a senior pastor who is driven to embrace people who are not in love with God. Whether we call it a gift, a passion or a calling, each pastor is unquestionably and unshakably committed to helping grow the Kingdom by attracting outsiders. Some of them are obviously brilliant; others are not. Some of them are charismatic; others are not. Some of them are experienced pastors; others are novices serving in their first church. But the fact that God's love and vision have been instilled within the hearts of these men (I am not being sexist—all of the pastors we interviewed happened to be male, as is true of 96 percent of the pastors of Protestant churches.)

We also found that each church anchors its efforts with a firm understanding of the scriptural imperative to reach the unreached. The pastors and staff we interviewed cited different passages of the Bible that moved them, but all of them referred to God's Word as the fundamental motivational factor that leads them to pursue those who are hard to reach.

Furthermore, in every church, this ministry is a church-wide crusade, not the pastor's pet project. The goal is to have everyone in the congregation take the initial steps to building bridges to unchurched people and to eventually invite those individuals to the church. Even the new churches we studied were characterized by the founding pastor enlisting the participation of a few core individuals who shared a passion for reaching unreached individuals. The philosophy was that this effort must be the driving purpose of the church, not just an ancillary ministry.

With these discoveries in mind, I will identify some of the keys to effective church-based ministry to the unchurched. Note that every one of the two dozen churches we studied in greater detail operates differently than every other one. What I will describe for you are the common philosophies and activities they share as well as some of their most effective practices.

BEST PRACTICES: PHILOSOPHY OF MINISTRY

The underlying purpose of these churches is clear to all who participate in them: To love people into the kingdom of God. While the leaders of these churches are cognizant of attendance figures, they are more concerned about hearts and souls. For them, reaching the unchurched is not just a numbers game. "I'd rather see 10 people come to the Lord and really grow into maturity than have an auditorium filled with happy faces but empty souls," said the pastor of a church in Iowa.

These successful churches focus on building God's kingdom, not the pastor's kingdom or the church's turf. The pastor of a Baptist church in Texas that regularly attracts 1,500 adults described his view: "One of the things we've learned is that God blesses your church with growth when you're not selfish about wanting to keep all of those people inside your building. It's amazing how God takes care of that!"

Using Scripture as the foundation, people in these churches also have a keen sense of their dependence upon the Holy Spirit to do the brunt of the work. The church, through its efforts and attitudes, creates an environment in which God can impact the minds and hearts of unchurched people. "When they come here, our goal is for them to sense the presence of God. We want every single person that comes in to respond to and connect with God," said one pastor. "It goes back to an old philosophy: the Holy Spirit will work in every single person we touch. The Holy Spirit led that person to our church because God wants to get to know them."

The laser-like focus of these churches is impossible to miss. "To a hammer, everything looks like a nail" is a common expression. Yet that is exactly what these churches are like. To them every unchurched person looks like a human being just waiting to have a transforming experience with God. Even the language they use to describe the unchurched—pre-Christians, people who do not yet realize God loves them, soon-to-be-Christians—reflects that view. "Evangelism is really the only thing we can do better here on Earth than we will in heaven," opined one pastor. "Once we get saved, it becomes our primary purpose for existence."

> Reaching the unchurched demands a persistent effort to remain culturally aware and relevant.

Another pastor echoed the same sentiment: "When you boil it all down, we do two things: evangelize and disciple people. So we create a place where God can work through us to do those things."

It is not that these individuals ignore the significance of worship, stewardship or community service; rather, they simply see evangelism and discipleship as the priorities, and everything else flows from those two foci.

Need to Be Relevant

Reaching the unchurched demands a persistent effort to remain culturally aware and relevant. "We continue to ask questions," a pastor explained about his church's ability to remain attractive to the unchurched. "This isn't a 'done' thing for us, and I don't think it ever will be. It's very dynamic. Society just keeps changing, so we have to stay in touch with the culture. We have to be willing to 'de-weird' the church."

This approach also means that a church's activities will be constantly changing and shifting to remain in step with the culture. One of the refreshing attitudes of the pastors we interviewed was their determination to experiment continually and to refuse to lock into one set approach. "We do whatever it takes" was the philosophy of the pastor of a church in Texas that has grown large and is pioneering a variety of new strategies to reaching people, such as starting mini-churches in retirement villages and apartment complexes as well as planting ethnic churches throughout the city. "We try all means to get someone in. We're willing to try anything," he added.

If constant change is to be a reality, it also means that church members will challenge their prevailing assumptions about almost everything. Conditions that used to be taken for granted are now up for grabs, so leaders have to be wary of falling into routines and ruts—even if those routines were trailblazers ten years ago. Pastors have even questioned the viability of building on basic knowledge that was once a safe assumption. "We're finding more and more people who have no Christian background, where even five or ten years ago everybody had grown up going to Sunday school, or the church down the street, or a vacation Bible school," said one pastor. This man leads a contemporary church in the middle of the South and has had to identify and reassess even his most basic beliefs about what people know and how they think. "The thing that's been hard for me to adjust to is that there are people that if I say, 'When Adam and Eve did so and so,' then I've got to stop purposely and explain who Adam and Eve were. But that's just part of the art of reaching these people; you can't figure they're just like you are," he added.

Steal and Adopt

One of the approaches that all of these churches accept is the "steal and adapt" strategy. "Hey, if you look closely at what we're doing—well, you don't even have to look that closely—there's not a whole lot that we do that's original or stellar. I mean, we're not a pioneering church," admitted one pastor. He leads an Evangelical Free church of 1,300-plus adults in Michigan and recognizes that a lifetime's worth of great ideas and ministry lessons are available to him from the other church leaders who share the same heartbeat to reach the unchurched. "We do some things well, we do some things poorly, and for some reason God has chosen to make this place explode, and so it does," he said. "We don't have secrets or hidden things that make us successful. We read constantly. We grab stuff from here and there. We tweak it a little here, twist it a little there, make it ours. But it is a collection of other people's stuff that we've just adapted, based on what they've learned and what we've experienced."

Sometimes this results in churched people losing their sense of comfort. One of the pastors, who heads a church in Alabama, responded, "The things we do put off some of my churched people, but we find that the unchurched say, 'Hey, we really want to check out a place like that.' We built this place to reach the unchurched, so if anyone has to feel uncomfortable here, I'm okay with it being the churched folk. They'll find a place that will keep them happy."

The underlying assumption is that if people who attend a church are excited about it, then their conviction and enthusiasm—not marketing gimmicks, sermon series, free gifts or Broadway productions—will capture the attention of their unchurched friends. The Alabama pastor added, "Bottom line? People like to go to church where somebody else likes to go to church. If people are going away from this place and gossiping that good things are happening here, that gets other folks interested. When church people get excited, other people want to know why."

The Excitement Principle

The outreach director at a Lutheran church found the excitement principle to be a key. But he also found that the enthusiasm had to be authentic, not manufactured, and the joy had to be present all week long, not only on Sundays. "I was in a church where we had a 40-foot stretch between the door to the worship center and the doorway into the sanctuary," he said. "We established a rule that a visitor needed to be greeted at least four times before they got into that sanctuary. And it worked! They were greeted every 10 feet. Except there was one little problem: That was not what the culture of the church was *really* like. Most of the people just stood along the outer walls of the church; they weren't enthusiastic about new people joining us. So a visitor would enter, get a warm and friendly greeting several times and then think, 'This is a pretty good church, let's join.' For a few weeks, until they become known, they were treated nicely and greeted warmly, but then they became part of the familiar crowd. They sort of settled in and all of a sudden they're looking around wondering, *What happened? Now I'm not important anymore?* And it was because we created a false culture. The people who really were the heart of the church just weren't interested in them. We had created a façade to the church, and it was really harmful."

The Importance of the Heart

Most of the pastors we spoke to discussed the importance of the heart of the people. "It's all about people. Your people have to have a heart to see others come to know Jesus and to connect with those people," one pastor told us. "You can do without books and tapes and seminars, but you can't make this kind of ministry happen without people that have that heart."

Perhaps more than anything else, ministry to the unchurched hinges on one core factor: relationships. This point was driven home to one pastor through the comments of some people who recently visited his church: "Yeah, it's funny because for five or six years we did radio advertising. Some of those people who heard the ads are coming now. But they never came when all they heard were the radio spots. Now, because a friend asked them to come, they're here. I ask them, 'When did you first hear about our church?' and they'll say, 'Oh, I used to listen to your radio spots all the time.' But it wasn't the radio that brought them to church. It introduced them to the church, but they didn't come until years later when their friend invited them."

A similar insight was conveyed from a different angle by a Baptist pastor in Northern California. "People don't want a friendly church. They want a friend. Systems don't work. You have to create ways to enable people to find a genuine friend."

The underlying philosophy of these ministries is that unless the people of the church truly care about the unchurched and are willing to make the sacrifices for those relationships to occur, the ministry is headed for disaster.

BEST PRACTICES: PREPARATION

A great ministry to the unchurched does not just happen. Such a ministry is not only the result of a clear, thoughtful and well-articulated philosophy but also a commitment to adequate preparation of the congregation. The pastors of these churches have worked long and hard to get people in the right frame of mind so that the ministry is not a bunch of programs, but a group of loving people who really care about the spiritual health of others. The leaders want their people to be always thinking about building relationships with unchurched people.

"It takes a long time for that to become part of their mind-set," cautioned one senior pastor. "Almost every week I weave the importance of sensitivity and reaching out and making friendships into the message and into our announcements. It's so easy for people to revert to their old ways. They need continual reminders that the old ways are not what we're about, not what God has called us to."

Training for Every Person

The goal is that when the churched invite the unchurched to accompany them to a service or other activity, that invitation is satisfying an expectation, not serving as an exception. The relationships remove big hurdles for churches to overcome: isolation and the fear of remaining disconnected.

But the people have to be prepared to discuss their faith, too. "If my people encounter an individual who is not a believer but really wants to know what this stuff is all about, I don't want them running to the church to drag the evangelism director out there to share the gospel," one pastor said. "That's why we don't have an evangelism director; every person in this place is an evangelism director."

For this reason apologetics becomes an essential focus within the church. "But that word is so—sophisticated!" retorted one pastor. "It's not really high-level stuff we're dealing with here. My people need to be ready to address all kinds of theological garbage that the unchurched have unwittingly bought into over the years. My people have to be prepared to give a clear and articulate reason for the hope and faith that is within them. We're not talking the Mannheim Lectures here; we're talking about being able to communicate the basic stories of the Bible and relate them to everyday life."

Having a strong ministry to the unchurched also takes resources. We found that successful churches intentionally and strategically budget funds to do this work. On average, about 20 percent of the annual church budget is geared to this specific process. Several pastors demurred, stating that everything the church does is geared to the unchurched and therefore their entire budget fits this category.

From Outsider to Insider

These model churches have worked hard to provide many ways that an outsider can easily become an insider. While the worship service gets most of the attention, many of the pastors recognize that it all starts with relationships and perhaps other exposure to the faith world before the unchurched individual sets foot inside the worship center.

"We joined the city sports leagues, we hold seminars, we do all kinds of bridging events," one successful pastor divulged. "We know they [the unchurched] are not going to be converted at those events—we don't even try, really. We just want them to know that we're nice, normal people; we struggle with the same issues; we have many of the same interests; but we have that little something extra—the Jesus factor—that gives us the edge. I don't care how they catch that notion, as long as they want more and more of it to be revealed. So we try all kinds of avenues that allow them to enter into a relationship with us and with God."

The Whole Picture

Ultimately, many of the unchurched attend a worship service, so these churches go to great lengths to ensure that their gatherings are worshipful while also being accessible to people who have little or no history in church. The choice of music—the lyrics, the instrumentation, the difficulty of the tunes—is important. The topics of the message and the language used are carefully considered. Integration of technology into the worship process—video clips, PowerPoint slides, excellent sound systems, good lighting—are part of the approach. The layout of the church campus, signage, comfort of the seating, ease of parking—all of these elements and more are painstakingly examined and constantly refined since they are an integral part of the aggregate experience. It is all considered part of the preparation for guiding the unchurched to God while also meeting the needs of the church family.

Best Practices: Process

The successful penetration of the ranks of the unchurched largely hinges on whether or not the congregants build credible relationships with people and then invite those friends to attend the church. This often means visiting a worship service. In the effective churches, anywhere between 40 and 85 percent of the members actually invite nonbelievers to attend during a typical year.

> About half of the highly effective churches use some form of advertising to get the word out, too.

Most of the effective churches strive to support their congregants in this effort by putting on from four to eight special events each year. Besides the usual seasonal events, they also host concerts, fairs, carnivals, artistic events, movie nights and other creative gatherings. The purpose of these events is to raise awareness and build a positive image of the church. The gatherings often help members ease an unchurched friend into contact with the ministry and its adherents. The churches that had used more traditional events—such as Vacation Bible School or handing out the *Jesus* video—found that those experiences were generally unproductive among the unchurched.

About half of the highly effective churches use some form of advertising to get the word out, too. Most of that advertising spotlights upcoming events. A few churches tried image advertising but found it difficult to justify the ongoing cost. Four out of every five of the effective churches that had tried radio advertising found it to be of limited value unless it was to promote an event. "People don't go to church because of clever radio ads. They may attend an event, for an entertaining experience, based on an ad, but attending church is a different ballpark," reported one pastor.

The Makeup of the Worship Service

Once we get the unchurched to church, the content of the worship service is crucial—but perhaps not in the ways usually assumed. As I have already noted, to unchurched people, the most important thing they derive from their visit is a feel for the people, not the substance of the church's beliefs and doctrine. (A piece of research we did several years ago indicated that most unchurched people don't really listen to the content of the sermon that closely during their first two or three visits, but they scrutinize very carefully the delivery, the tone, the audience reaction and both the speaker's and congregation's body language.)

The worship services, therefore, are designed to allow believers truly to connect with God in a context that is culturally relevant and uplifting. The unchurched, who probably cannot distinguish authentic worship from a blueberry bagel, are scoping out the situation from their own, less-informed vantage point. So they notice that the music is fun but substantive. The dramas or videos are often humorous but poignant. The big-screen visuals make following and learning from the message lively and helpful. The sermon outline included in the program reinforces the importance of the message while it also facilitates recall of the content. The Bible version that is used is a contemporary translation, with copies readily available to those who do not have a Bible with them. The length of the sermons, the topics addressed, the manner of presentation—all of those elements have been thought through to result in a dynamic presentation.

Identifying the Visitors

These churches are completely comfortable with allowing visitors total anonymity for as long as they want to remain undercover. But once a visitor identifies himself or herself as a newcomer, a carefully conceived, multistage interaction process is triggered. In every service each attendee is asked to fill out a response device of some type. Each church has a well-conceived and carefully carried out process once a visitor submits that information. The process itself differs from church to church, of course, but here is a fairly common approach.

1. The pastor or other church leaders are available to meet with visitors after the service in a designated area. There is no pressure on newcomers to take advantage of this "meet and greet" opportunity; rather, during the service there is just a casual mention that these individuals will be accessible.

2. Within 48 hours of the service, the pastor will send a letter of thanks to the visitor. In the letter, the pastor will encourage the visitor to return and invite him or her to call if he or she has any needs or questions.

3. Within five days of having attended the worship service, the visitor will get a call from someone at the church—often the pastor. The caller will thank the visitor for coming to church and ask if he or she has any questions.

4. If the visitor does not return, the church continues to send mailings, usually for at least a year. Generally these mailings will announce upcoming special events.

5. If the individual comes to a second service or event, then the church becomes more aggressive, either sending someone to the person's home (big in the South, not as common elsewhere), making a phone call or sending another targeted letter. The idea at this stage is to get the person integrated into the life of the church. He or she is invited to attend a newcomer's class. The visitor is also likely to receive several invitations during the weeks following his or her second visit.

6. If the person attends the newcomer's class, then a primary outcome is to get him or her involved in a service ministry. (Yes, a newcomer can serve in the church before he or she is saved. I will explain later in this chapter.)

We heard countless variations on this theme. There are special welcome or introductory dinners, home visitation and gift drop-off programs, e-mail messages, pastoral visitation, contacts by small group leaders and other creative approaches. The most common stream of activity, though, is what I have outlined above.

Getting the Visitor Involved

One key to the process is to get the newcomer involved as quickly as possible after they fill out a card. "We discovered that a lot of people won't fill out the card until they've been here three or four times," shared one pastor. "So we figure, OK, once you fill it out, that probably means you're ready to take the next step, and we want to make that easy for them. We make sure they get contacted several times in the next few weeks—nothing high pressure, just letting them know that we care, that we're available, that there are opportunities if they're interested."

Why the rush to move them into a more intense connection with the church? Because most of these churches have learned that if a person is not integrated or connected to the life of the church through serving others or through a connectional ministry (e.g., a class or small group), then the chances are very high of them not getting connected at all.

At the same time, this calls for deft judgment and patience. A church can easily become too aggressive and, no matter how well-intentioned, chase off an interested but cautious explorer. "We find a lot of people come once or twice or three times, maybe go away and then come back again in three or four months," the associate pastor of a large church in the Cincinnati area said. "Becoming churched is a process, you know? So we try not to scare them off. We want them to feel like they can come back and try this place for as long as they like."

There is a fine line between allowing people to get involved at their own pace and losing the window of opportunity. "Some people don't want to be pursued," one church leader told us. "There's a certain level of anonymity that is important for most unchurched people. In some ways, giving them the space to control the situation works well, but in other ways it obviously hinders our ability to follow up effectively. Sometimes they're waiting on us; other times, they're wary of us. It's hard to know what the proper balance is. We pray and believe God will guide us in these instances."

Most of the pastors we interviewed stressed the significance of the assimilation process. Merely getting people to attend services or become members, or even to make a commitment to Christ, was not deemed to be a sufficient outcome. "We feel like we have six weeks to connect them with somebody or else they'll drift away or stay in the shadows" was one comment that represented the feelings of many people we interviewed. "We try to get them into the life of the church as fast as they're moving, you know? We don't have a timetable for that; we're trying to be both patient and not negligent. We try to hit that balance by offering encouragement, direction and opportunities. At the same time, we try not to coerce or pressure them."

The Problem of Success

One of the most obvious conflicts that has gripped these churches is that between attraction and assimilation. "Our ability to attract people far outstrips our ability to minister to them in deep ways," admitted one pastor. "I just can't seem to train people fast enough to keep up with the demand. The more successful we are at reaching the unchurched, the bigger the challenge we have in developing mature followers."

This problem seems to become more pronounced the larger the church gets. The leader of a congregation of 6,000 people described the paradox: "Our problem isn't attracting them; we've grown pretty fast. The problem is having structures and seeing people get involved and looking after them. We don't feel we can slow down the front end, so what are we going to do? Hang out a shingle that says, 'Sorry, we're full. Everybody else, go to hell.' Can't do that! So you do your best as people come in and keep trying to improve your structures."

BEST PRACTICES: PRODUCTS

What does "success" look like at churches that strive to reach the unchurched? Surprisingly, there was not a lot of agreement on this matter.

The most common answers we received were the following:

- baptisms
- increased numbers of people in small groups
- more people involved in serving others
- a high percentage of new members who are not joining by transfer
- people indicating they have accepted Christ as their Savior
- consistent attendance at worship services
- completion of the newcomer's class

I was intrigued by some of the factors that were not mentioned. For instance, not one of the pastors noted the percentage of people in the church who invite unchurched people (most of the pastors had no idea what that figure currently is among their people) or increased knowledge of the basic principles of Christianity. Perhaps this was an oversight on their part, or maybe they felt that those outcomes were subsumed under other outcomes they had already mentioned.

All of these results, along with the handful of others that were cited, relate to transformation. A pastor from Nevada stated the goal most clearly: "Our church is successful when people come to know Jesus Christ as their Savior and Lord and when their lives are changed. If people's lives aren't being changed by an encounter with the almighty God and their families transformed and their communities impacted, then we've not made a difference. At the end of 5 or 10 years, our community better have changed by our presence or else I will really question the efficacy of what we've done. If it's simply a lot of people who said, 'Yeah, I prayed the prayer,' but their families didn't change and the community is not impacted, then I will really question the ultimate success of our mission here."

MORE INSIGHTS

In closing out this summary of what the most effective churches do to reach and retain the unchurched, let me relay eight additional bits of wisdom imparted by the pastors of these model churches.

If your church is not attracting unchurched people, you're probably not ready to handle it.

Although it is not a popular notion, sometimes churches fail to attract the unchurched because God is protecting both the church and the unchurched from exposure to each other. As we have seen, successful ministry to the unchurched takes more than just getting them inside the sanctuary. A pastor from New York expressed this idea well. "God doesn't bring an increase if you can't handle it," he said. "If we're not prepared to take care of those who are evangelized, whether that's in the area of discipleship or getting them involved in ministry or whatever, God is too smart to bring the increase. Our job as church leaders is to put ourselves in positions where we're doing our part of the job. When numbers have slowed, in membership and conversions, that's always been a sign to me that something we're doing needs to be assessed and we need to prepare ourselves better for the next level of ministry."

If people start coming from other churches, that is a mixed blessing.

If word gets around that your church is a special place, then you will probably start to attract many unchurched people—as well as many churched individuals. There are millions of Christians who habitually move from church to church, striving to be at the "hot" church in town. The influx of these people is generally a double-edged sword. On the one hand, their presence is a blessing because it is a sign that good word-of-mouth promotion is happening on behalf of your church. Sometimes these people are mature Christians who add value to your ministry. On the other hand, their presence is often seen as a curse because they are more interested in being entertained or coddled than in growing and serving. The church typically runs a net loss in terms of ministry health as a result of their attendance because these people absorb more of the church's resources than they invest in the ministry.

You are not called to reach the world, only a portion of it.

This statement will upset a number of people who interpret the Great Commission to mean that they are called to reach all nonbelievers. But that interpretation is neither accurate nor reasonable. Several of the pastors of the effective churches are cautious in how they use Matthew 28. One such pastor put it this way: "I want to be faithful to God's calling to me and to this church, but that calling is not for us to reach the entire world. That's the job of the Church worldwide. My immediate task is to try to share the gospel with every person near our church, though—and that's a daunting enough challenge. If I try to convince my people that we're supposed to win the entire world, they'll walk away, knowing that it's too big a challenge. But if I can give them a mission they can accept as reasonable—big, challenging, unprecedented, sure; but within the scope of reason—they'll climb on board."

In other words, the challenges we pose to our people must be achievable.

Recognize that churched and unchurched people have similar needs and dissimilar needs.

No, that is not double-talk. That is a description of the magnitude of the challenge that faces any church that straddles the fence between the churched and unchurched. Every person has similar needs—love, comfort, security, belonging, food, clothing, shelter and more. But the factors on which each group bases its selection of a church differ. Churched people seek a broad slate of strong programs along with challenging preaching and desirable music. The unchurched search for a grip on reality and personal applications. The churched want an organization of which they can be proud. The unchurched want relationships with people who are genuine and caring. The churched want to improve their church situation. The unchurched desire to improve their quality of life.

The healthier your church is, the less of a problem leakage will be.

Many churches that dabble in ministry to the unchurched become discouraged because so few of the visitors return and get involved. One secret to alleviating this problem is to be sure the people in your church have healthy spiritual lives. If they do, then they will have a heart for the unchurched and will acquire the tools with which to minister to them. If a church reaches many but retains few, then it needs to evaluate the health of its congregants. In all likelihood the church has a people problem, not a program deficiency.

Unsaved people can serve—and everyone can profit from the experience.

Thousands of churches refuse to let unchurched people get involved in the ministry until they make a firm commitment to follow Christ. Most of the effective churches took a different stand. They identified certain tasks that people could perform that enabled them to get involved and feel useful and encouraged them to attend more regularly. "You don't need to have accepted Christ to serve coffee or park cars or stuff programs," stated one pastor we spoke to. "I can't let them teach, but getting them to serve is a great step toward becoming a mature believer. I want to form that habit in them as soon as possible; letting them come and sit around watching us do ministry every week is simply not healthy, even for a fence-sitter."

Standardized developmental tools are important but not paramount.

Frankly, I was surprised that a larger share of these churches did not use many of the resources and tools that have been created for use by churches. For instance, although many of these churches try to incorporate people into small groups as soon as possible, relatively few of the churches use the same small group materials. The Alpha course has been a viable tool for thousands of churches overseas, but only two of the effective churches that we examined in the United States use it and less than a half dozen had even heard of it. The Internet is essentially an untapped tool; most of the churches have a website, but nothing specifically geared to help or reach an unchurched person. Virtually every newcomer's class is based on self-developed material. There is no standard procedure or material used to gather information from people who visit and never return. Yet all of these churches are doing a terrific job. Maybe they could do an even better job if they used productive tools, but certainly the lesson is that having an impact in people's lives is dependent upon passion, prayer and people more than materials.

Ministering to the unchurched is serious spiritual business.

Anyone who delves into ministry to those who have little, if any, involvement with God must plan to encounter intense spiritual challenges. The strategic transition of people from darkness to faith in Christ will stir up the powers of evil and generate stiff spiritual opposition. As the pastors of these model churches indicated, those who want to reach the unchurched must be prepared to fight a difficult battle for the hearts, minds and souls of these individuals. We must take Paul's advice and put on the full armor of God as we pursue the unchurched. Our ministry to them is a battle call to the enemy.

CHAPTER 11

MAKING A COMMITMENT TO A VISION OF THE CHURCH

What are we striving to accomplish when we gather the saints and soon-to-be saints together? Our goal must be more than just filling up the sanctuary or sustaining a menu full of ministry programs. This is where the importance of leadership comes into play. As we read through the book of Acts, it becomes clear that individuals emerged—Peter, James and Paul, for instance—who had been called by God to influence those who asked, "What shall we do?" In the hearts and minds of those appointed individuals—His chosen leaders—He instilled a vision of how to move forward with the development of the Church. That vision is His blueprint that we can follow to experience the fullness of the life He has given to us.

If you are a leader called by God to move His Church forward, His vision is the cornerstone of your leadership. Communicate it clearly and persuasively to everyone who will listen, as often as you have the opportunity. Convey that vision in such a compelling manner that people can envision a future in which people's lives are being transformed to be more Christlike and in ways in which every individual can play a meaningful role. Pray for opportunities to share that vision, for people who will hear it and embrace it, for the resources to make it happen and for the ability to direct people's efforts efficiently and effectively.

If you are a follower of Christ but not called to such a leadership position, then listen carefully to the vision that is being cast by His chosen leaders and embrace the vision as if it were your own. Commit to it. Use your gifts and resources to fulfill it. Pray about the vision, about your role in bringing it to pass and about God's willingness to use you in significant ways to reach the world for His glory. Listen and watch for His response to your prayers.

COMMIT TO PEOPLE

Strange as it may seem, God chose to work through human beings to glorify Himself. In my less profound moments—and they are legion!—I look at myself and other people and conclude that the creation of humanity was not one of God's inspired choices. But a careful read through His Word emphasizes that we are both an inspired and exciting creation. You and I have a chance to know the Creator intimately and to be part of His kingdom, doing special works of service that He set aside for each one of us. What an incredible opportunity!

Analyze His exhortations to us and you will find that His challenges are all about how we work with people. Organizational structures and operational systems have a place in the larger scheme of things, but the reason for their existence is to build up people. Our energy must be poured into people.

But how can we do that in a meaningful way? There are so many needs and we easily get overwhelmed or sidetracked. What can we do to make a difference?

Working by ourselves, outside a community of believers who are committed to a vision from God and directions from His chosen leader, perhaps we *cannot* do much. That is why it is imperative that we work as a team—or, in religious parlance, as a church—to maximize our capacity to facilitate positive change in people's lives.

Of course, this sounds high-minded when described in such prosaic terms, but the reality is that being a church which follows God's vision is all about the details of Scripture and the implementation of change. It relates to marketing, communications, training, fund-raising, counseling, administration and all that goes along with that. Somehow those endeavors seem less holy and inspiring than talk about vision and the imitation of Christ. But they are one and the same. We cannot get from here to there without such efforts.

> **K**eep our goal in mind: It is not to build a perfect church but to honor the perfect Creator.

Keep our goal in mind: It is not to build a perfect church but to honor the perfect Creator. Our efforts must include our call to worship Him, to know Him and to know about Him and His ways. It must involve our service to Him and His people. The actual structure of the church does not really matter to God. If it did, He would have given us a detailed outline of what it must look like, just as He gave Noah exact measurements for the ark. But He did not provide such a blueprint because He is more interested in the state of our hearts than in the size of our buildings or the design of our organizations.

GET PRACTICAL

If you are at all like me, the preceding paragraphs may seem like a preamble to the "real stuff," the nuts and bolts of how we make the Church work. Without minimizing the significance of vision, teamwork and perspective, let me briefly address some of the details that may be part of the developmental process.

Model It

Our research reveals a lot about the unchurched. Without question, their disinterest in the Church is partly because Christians have not adequately represented God. Once we clean up our act, our lives will become a pleasing fragrance not just to the Lord but also to those around us on Earth. We may also help reduce their confusion by offering them distinct options to pursue, such as churches that approach faith through different styles and emphases, but without ever compromising Scripture or ignoring the foundations of the Church.

Distinctives

In our communications with the unchurched, we must remember that while relationships are important in building a church, those whom we want to attract are a less relational group of people. Relationships will only get us so far with them. They still require a clear understanding of our USP (that's the business world's abbreviation for "Unique Selling Proposition"). In other words, what is it that we have to offer that is different and valuable in the eyes of the target audience?

What they are looking for is a better life. Can you lead them to a place or to a group of people that will deliver the building blocks of a better life? Do not propose Christianity as a system of rules but as a relationship with the One who leads by way of example. Then seek proven ways to achieve meaning and success. Christianity provides that—and along the way it redefines what those terms mean.

Keep in mind that as you describe that better life and how well it has worked for you, the proof is in the experience: They do not want to hear about the Christian life or the joy of faith; they want to observe it in you and your churched colleagues.

Be on guard against making unrealistic claims such as "Your life will never be the same," "You'll have a new family that loves you deeply," "You'll never be alone" or "You've never experienced anything like this." No matter how true these assertions may be, they are not immediately credible, unless your life is a crystal clear demonstration of those very realities. Appeal to the unchurched in believable terms, and allow God to overwhelm them with His ability to deliver promises that are even bigger and better than we could ever make.

Substance

We lose our opportunity to connect with many unchurched individuals long before they visit a worship service. The reason is that we have not read them well. They require control, independence and choices. In a church, we generally require submission, not just to Jesus but also to the dictates of the church. There is a natural conflict here—but it is not irreconcilable. If we are comfortable with and confident in our faith, then we can ask ourselves if there are ways that we can allow people who support liberal ideas, such as hypertolerance and relativism, to be in our midst. We can open the door so that they can hear and experience God's truths, without immediately stripping them of their predispositions. I am not making a call to compromise, for that would bring defeat. The call is for us to guide the unchurched into God's kingdom through love, understanding and diligence.

EXPLOIT ALL OPPORTUNITIES

It seems that we may not be taking advantage of all the opportunities available to us. I am surprised by three conditions in particular.

First, as I have already noted, we do not seem to be exploiting the possibilities available to us through the Internet. Having a church website is nice, but that is passive marketing. Too many churches put something on a site and then hope that those who need the information will find it through some unpredictable and ill-defined search process. Are there more creative, aggressive and intentional ways of connecting with unchurched people to bring them into a deeper relationship with Jesus? Our research shows that a growing portion of the population is open to, if not actively seeking, online opportunities to engage with God and His people. A passive church website will not do it. But if we build a virtual church on the Internet, it may reach an entire segment of the unchurched that is otherwise inaccessible.

Second, I was also surprised by the predictability of the churches that are successfully reaching the unchurched. Without meaning to disparage any of those churches—they are doing a great job and the Body of Christ is blessed by their presence and their example—I wonder if there are not significantly different models of faith expression and community that could be created to reach this target market.

We know, for instance, that churched people are already clamoring for (and respond favorably to) new models of the church. The congregational format that we have used for hundreds of years in churches does not really fit our culture very well, so new models (house churches, marketplace ministries and cyberchurches) are attractive to a growing number of people. Most of these models are being developed for disgruntled churchgoers. What would some new models look like for the unchurched? Who will have the courage to take the risk of experimenting with these models?

Third, it is surprising that we do not focus more energy on reaching children as our primary outreach thrust. Perhaps because we are adults, it is our natural inclination to focus on people like ourselves. However, the research is very clear: People do not change much, they do not strive to change much and if Jesus is not already part of their lives by the time they leave high school, the chances of their accepting Him as their Lord and Savior are very slim (6 percent, to be exact). With children, it's just the opposite. Because of the challenges and insecurities they face in life, they are very open to being part of a community of like-minded people who grow together. We also know that children have tremendous influence within their families—on spending patterns, on entertainment choices, on relationships and even on matters of faith.

Of the churches we interviewed that are most effective at reaching the unchurched, only one had children as a primary target group. We did not speak to every church leader in America who is effective at reaching the unchurched. I realize that there are probably many churches that target kids. But the evidence suggests that we typically think about adults first and assume the kids will tag along. Perhaps the reverse strategy would be true: A more concentrated effort at reaching kids would bring more adults (i.e., their parents) along for the ride. In fact, a more targeted effort at reaching kids might revolutionize the future church, when these kids are grown and needed as the church's leaders. Rather than having to reinterest them in the Church, perhaps their experience during their formative years would result in a positive reengineering of the Church to incorporate their generation.

SEE THE HEART OF JESUS

One section of the Bible often comes to mind as I think about the unchurched. It deals with Jesus' reaction to the crowds who followed Him, who were searching for hope and answers. The Bible repeatedly describes how Jesus had compassion for the people because they were needy and helpless—like "sheep without a shepherd" (Matt. 9:36).

If you're like me, you have no trouble keeping yourself busy from moment to moment. One consequence of having a jammed schedule is that I often lack the ability to see the crowd the way Jesus saw it and to realize that Jesus has called each one of us, even me, to have compassion on those who are searching for meaning and purpose in life. My prayer is that I might have the heart of Jesus for those people. It is my prayer for you, too.

There are almost 100 million people living in our own country who are not connected to a church. Millions and millions of them desperately seek a meaningful faith connection. You know some of them. What will you do to meet their needs?

RESEARCH METHODOLOGY

This book is based upon a number of research efforts related to the unchurched and churches that minister effectively to them. Here is an outline of the research projects conducted by the Barna Research Group from which the data were derived.

SURVEYS AMONG ADULTS

All of the following were telephone surveys based upon nationwide random samples of adults living in the 48 continental states. The surveys were conducted from the Barna Research field center in Southern California, and interviews were conducted on week nights from 5:00 P.M. to 9:00 P.M., on Saturdays from 10:00 A.M. to 6:00 P.M. and on Sundays from noon through 8:00 P.M. (all times listed are the times in the time zone of the survey respondent). Unchurched adults were defined as those who had not attended a church service within the past six months, other than for a special event such as a wedding or funeral.

Completed interviews among the:

Survey field dates	Churched	Unchurched
January-February 1999	750	282
April-May 1999	0	601
July-August 1999	727	273
November-December 1999	723	230
January-February 2000	675	327
May-June 2000	681	322

SURVEYS AMONG PASTORS

In addition to interviewing churched and unchurched adults, we also spoke with two samples of senior pastors of Protestant churches. One survey was a national random sampling of 601 senior pastors, conducted by telephone during June 2000 and July 2000. That survey was a representative sampling of Protestant churches and included questions that pertained to ministry to the unchurched.

The other study was among an elite sample of pastors and church leaders from congregations that have done an outstanding job of reaching the unchurched. The original sample list was developed from calls made to denominational executives, church consultants and analysts and ministry specialists. From that list we then narrowed down the body of qualified churches to those who are doing unusually effective ministry among the unchurched. That was determined by assessing the percentage of unchurched visitors the church attracts and retains each year, the ministry emphasis placed upon reaching unchurched people and the number of changed lives that have resulted from such ministry. This portion of the research was qualitative and nonstatistical in nature, based upon extensive interviews and evaluations of the church's efforts to reach and relate to unchurched people. The churches involved in this portion of the research came from every region of the country, represented more than a dozen Protestant denominations (mainline and evangelical) and ran from as few as 175 to as many as 6,000 adults attending the church on a typical weekend.

ADDITIONAL RESEARCH

This book also draws from information gathered in other surveys we have conducted. Among them is a nationwide telephone survey of a random sample of 610 teenagers conducted in October 1999. Allusions are made to research we conducted in 1990, 1993 and 1995 among the unchurched, using those data for comparative purposes. Each of those studies was a national telephone survey among a random sample of unchurched adults, ranging in size from 307 to 602 completed interviews among the unchurched.

About George Barna

George Barna is the president of the Barna Research Group, Ltd., a marketing research firm located in Ventura, California. The company specializes in conducting primary research for Christian ministries and nonprofit organizations. Since its inception in 1984, Barna Research has served several hundred parachurch ministries and numerous churches, in addition to various nonprofit and for-profit organizations.

Barna has written 32 books. His most recent works are *A Fish Out of Water, Boiling Point, The State of the Church: 2002, Real Teens* and *Single Adults*. Past works include best-sellers such as *The Frog in the Kettle, The Second Coming of the Church, User Friendly Churches, Marketing the Church* and *The Power of Vision*. Several of his books have received national awards. He has also written for numerous periodicals and has published more than two dozen syndicated reports on a variety of topics related to ministry. His work is frequently cited as an authoritative source by the media.

Barna is also widely known for his intensive, research-based seminars for church leaders. He is a popular speaker at ministry conferences around the world and has taught at several universities and seminaries. He has served as a pastor of a large, multiethnic church and has served on several boards of directors.

After graduating summa cum laude in sociology from Boston College, Barna earned two masters degrees from Rutgers University. He also received a doctorate from Dallas Baptist University.

He lives with his wife, Nancy, and their two daughters, Samantha and Corban, in Southern California. He enjoys spending time with his family, writing, reading, playing basketball and guitar, relaxing on the beach and visiting bookstores.

ABOUT THE BARNA RESEARCH GROUP, LTD.

The Barna Research Group, Ltd. (BRG) is a full-service marketing research company located in Ventura, California. BRG has been providing information and analysis regarding cultural trends, ministry practices, marketing and business strategy, fund-raising, worldviews and leadership since 1984. The vision of the company is to provide Christian ministries with current, accurate and reliable information in bite-sized pieces and at affordable prices, to facilitate effective and strategic decision making.

BRG conducts both quantitative and qualitative research using a variety of data collection methods, with particular emphasis upon the application of the results. The company conducts more research within the Christian community than any other organization in the United States and regularly releases reports describing its findings regarding the values, attitudes, lifestyles, religious beliefs and religious practices of adults and teenagers, as well as the current state of churches. That information is also accessible through the seminars, books, website, videotapes and audiotapes produced by BRG.

To access many of the findings of BRG, visit the company's website at www.barna.org. You will have access to the free bimonthly reports (*The Barna Update*) published on the site; a data archives that provides current statistics in relation to 40 aspects of ministry and lifestyle; the various resources produced by George Barna and the Barna Research Group; and information about upcoming seminars as well as the firm's research activities. If you wish to receive *The Barna Update* by e-mail every two weeks, you may sign up for that free service on the home page of their site.

To contact the Barna Research Group, call 805-658-8885 or write to 5528 Everglades Street, Ventura, CA 93003.

WHAT KIND OF LEADER ARE YOU? TAKE THE CHRISTIAN LEADER PROFILE AND FIND OUT!

Have you ever wondered if you are a leader, and if you are, how you measure up?

Now there is a diagnostic tool that will help you understand your leadership capacity more clearly. The Christian Leader Profile was developed by George Barna through extensive research and testing over several years. The Profile is designed to help you discern God's calling upon you as a leader and the nature of your leadership capacity by exploring four dimensions of leadership:

1. Has God **called you** to lead people?
   Every Christian who leads fulfills that role and responsibility solely because God calls them to that role. Has He called you?

2. Do you possess the **godly character** required of Christian leaders?
   1 Timothy 3 teaches that in addition to God's calling, a Christian leader must possess appropriate character. We're

not called to have perfect character, but character counts! How's your character?

3. What are your strongest and weakest **leadership competencies**?
   Of the dozen-plus core competencies that leaders must possess to be effective, which are your strongest and weakest capabilities, and how do those affect your ability to lead people?

4. What **type of leader** are you?
   Every leader is designed to provide one facet of a group's leadership. Which of the four leadership aptitudes—Directing, Strategic, Team-Building or Operational—do you represent?

It's easy and convenient to take advantage of this tool. Just log on to the Barna Research Group website home page (www.barna.org) and hit the icon to the Christian Leader Profile. You will be able to take the self-administered survey online and a personalized analysis of your results will be e-mailed to you within 48 hours of submitting your answers to the Profile's questions. Your analysis will clarify your standing as a leader and suggest future courses of action to enhance your impact for Christ through the ministry of leadership. This diagnostic tool will help you lead with greater confidence and focus.

Be the leader that God intends you to be.
The Christian Leader Profile will help you
become that leader.

A GLANCE AT THE UNCHURCHED

Some Useful Facts from Barna Research Group, Ltd.

Definition of the Unchurched: A person who has not attended a Christian church in the last six months, other than weddings, baptisms or other special events.

- Two-thirds of all Americans believe that the purpose of life is to enjoy blessings and gain the maximum fulfillment from their options and temptations.
- If all of the unchurched people in the United States were a nation of their own, they would be the eleventh most populated country on Earth.
- In mid-2000 about 95 to 100 million Americans of all ages were unchurched.
- Encountering hypocritical Christians is what the unchurched like least about their past experiences at church. They also do not like the strict or inflexible belief systems.
- The unchurched say the main reason they do not attend church is because they do not have the time.
- Most people who accept Christ as Savior do so between the ages of 5 and 13.
- Most of the unchurched (91 percent) describe themselves as self-sufficient and say they like to try new experiences (81 percent).
- More unchurched (65 percent) are satisfied with their marriages than Christians (59 percent) are satisfied with theirs.
- Three-fourths of the unchurched believe that God helps those who help themselves, even though this principle came from

Ben Franklin and is not biblical.

- Only 45 percent of the unchurched say they are searching for meaning in life.
- The unchurched prefer to be called inquirers or explorers. They do not want to be called lost.
- How much the people in a church seem to care about each other is the most important factor for the unchurched when selecting a church.
- Unchurched people are more likely to respond to a personal invitation than they are to surrender to pressure to belong to a group.

Feel free to duplicate this list and distribute it to the members of your church. It may help them better understand and reach out to the unchurched in your community.

For information about the unchurched visit www.barna.org.

BIBLIOGRAPHY

Barna, George. *Evangelism That Works*. Ventura, CA: Regal Books, 1995.

——. *Growing True Disciples*. Ventura, CA: Issachar Resources, 2000.

——. *The Habits of Highly Effective Churches*. Ventura, CA: Regal Books, 2000.

——. *Never On A Sunday*. Ventura, CA: Barna Research Group, 1990.

——. *The Second Coming of the Church*. Nashville: Word Books, 1998.

Barna, George and Hatch, Mark, *Boiling Point*. Ventura, CA: Regal Books, 2001.

Colson, Charles and Pearcey, Nancy, *How Now Shall We Live?* Wheaton, IL: Tyndale House Publishers, 1999.

Hoffecker, W. Andrew, ed. *Building A Christian World View, Vol. 1*. Phillipsburg, NJ: Presbyterian and Reformed Publishing Company, 1986.

Krueger, Otto and Thuesen, Janet, *Type Talk*. New York: Delta Books, 1989.

U.S. Bureau of the Census. *Statistical Abstract of the United States, 1999*. Prepared by the Economics and Statistics Administration in cooperation with the United States Department of Commerce, Bureau of the Census. Washington, DC, 1999.

MAKING THE GRADE AT BARNA UNIVERSITY

Become the Leader You Are Meant to Be

TRAINING FOR LEADERSHIP–BY LEADERS, FOR LEADERS, THROUGH BARNA UNIVERSITY

Would you like to receive the best leadership training available? Would you like your teachers to be some of the nation's finest practitioners in ministry leadership? Would you like that training to be delivered at a reasonable cost to your place of work?

If so, Barna University was created with you in mind!

In conjunction with CCN (Church Communication Network), Barna University provides learning sessions each year through satellite and Internet technology. Each session is taught by an experienced, highly regarded practitioner whose track record underscores his expertise. The emphasis of each session will be developing the skills and insights that every leader needs in order to be effective. In addition to the unique, interactive, satellite-delivered teaching sessions, you will have the following benefits:

- Online readings, references and application exercises
- A bulletin board for interaction with other students
- Continuing education units from accredited institutions
- Discounts on related products

Barna University's "revolving faculty" includes many of the nation's most dynamic Christian leaders. The annual enrollment fee is just a fraction of what you would pay in registration, travel and expenses if you were to attend similar seminars featuring these leaders. Barna University is more than great education; it's good stewardship, too.

If you would like more information about how to grow into the leadership shoes that God has provided for you, visit the Barna Research Group home page (www.barna.org) and click on the Barna University icon.

BARNA UNIVERSITY
HELPING YOU BECOME THE LEADER GOD INTENDED YOU TO BE.